THE GREENPEACE
TO AMCHITKA

THE GREENPEACE
TO AMCHITKA

An Environmental Odyssey

Robert Hunter

WITH PHOTOGRAPHS BY ROBERT KEZIERE

ARSENAL
PULP PRESS
Vancouver

ARSENAL PULP PRESS
103 - 1014 Homer Street
Vancouver, B.C.
Canada v6b 2w9
arsenalpulp.com

The publisher gratefully acknowledges the support of the Canada Council for the Arts and the British Columbia Arts Council for its publishing program, and the Government of Canada through the Book Publishing Industry Development Program for its publishing activities.

Edited by Mary Schendlinger
Design by Solo

Printed and bound in Canada

Library and Archives Canada
Cataloguing in Publication

   Hunter, Robert, 1941-
   The Greenpeace to Amchitka : an environmental odyssey / Robert
   Hunter ; photographs by Robert Keziere.

   Includes bibliographical references and index.
   ISBN 1-55152-178-4

   1. Hunter, Robert, 1941 – Journeys. 2. Keziere, Robert – Journeys.
   3. Greenpeace (Boat) 4. Greenpeace Foundation – History. I. Keziere, Robert
   II. Title.

   GE195.H86 2004   333.72   C2004-902955-X

This book was printed on recycled paper made with post-consumer waste; 12 trees, 1,073 pounds of solid waste, 1,180 gallons of water, and 1,540 kilowatt hours of electricity were saved as a result.

For Alex, Chaz, Dexter, and Rhys
who got to be born

We were so busy preparing to go to the moon
that we were completely unprepared for the
impact the trip would have on our lives.

– Astronaut Buzz Aldrin,
February 27, 1972

Contents

Before   15

During
    Gulf of Alaska   23
    Akutan   85
    Sand Point   139
    Home   197

After   233

Acknowledgments   239

RUSSIA

*Bering
Sea*

Amchitka Island

Aleutian Islands

International Date Line

Arctic Circle

United States
Canada

Fairbanks

Anchorage

Kodiak

Cape St Elias

*Gulf of
Alaska*

Juneau

Ketchikan

Dixon Entrance

Queen Charlotte Islands
Haida Gwaii

Prince Rupert

Klemtu

*Queen
Charlotte
Sound*

Bella Coola

Calvert Island

Vancouver
Island

Alert Bay

Comox

Strait of Georgia

Vancouver

Victoria

CANADA

Seattle

UNITED STATES

N

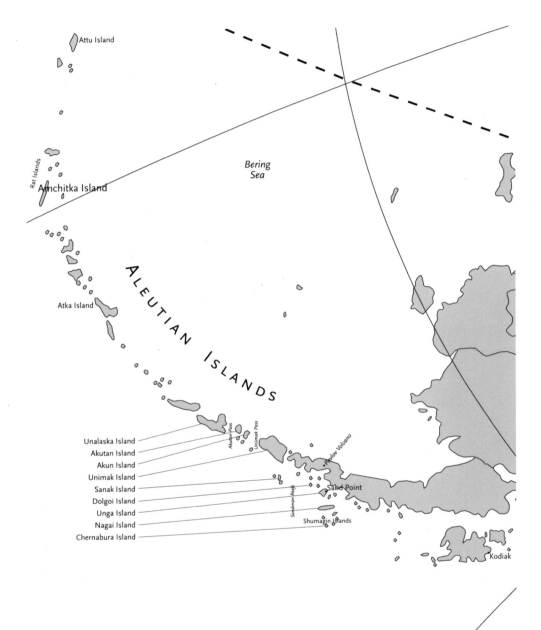

Attu Island

Rat Islands

Amchitka Island

Bering
Sea

A L E U T I A N   I S L A N D S

Atka Island

Unalaska Island
Akutan Island
Akun Island
Unimak Island
Sanak Island
Dolgoi Island
Unga Island
Nagai Island
Chernabura Island

Akutan Pass

Unimak Pass

Pavlov Volcano

Sand Point

Sandman Reefs

Shumagin Islands

Kodiak

Gulf of
Alaska

N →

BEFORE

The *Phyllis Cormack/Greenpeace* departs Vancouver on September 15, 1971.

Greenpeace was a product of the Vietnam War, as much as anything. The precursor to Greenpeace, the Don't Make a Wave Committee, was founded in 1970, at a time when no issue could stir up a crowd in Vancouver like 'Nam. The city was sheltering the largest American expatriate crowd in the world, resolutely anti-war to the last love child among them. This was a generation ago, back when TV showed the boys coming home from Southeast Asia in body bags, the after-image of Woodstock was still burned into the public's retina, the last of the Black Panthers were being gunned down, the *Eagle* had just landed on the moon, some 56,000 nuclear warheads were ready to be fired, a senility case ruled the Kremlin, and Richard Nixon was on speed in the White House. If you weren't paranoid, you were crazy.

In fact, the protest against the War was the counterculture's big-crowd ticket to media glory, having surpassed even Civil Rights as a *cause célèbre*, although the gunshots that took the lives of Martin Luther King Jr. and Bobby Kennedy were still echoing in our ears. The ecology movement, then known as conservationism, was a weak cousin of The Movement, as the hundreds of anti-establishment groups collectively were called, but the conservationists had also kept themselves apart deliberately. More than a few of them looked upon the American action in Vietnam with favour, and historically, such wonders as national parks had been a Republican cause. The organizers of the Don't Make a Wave Committee were Jim Bohlen and Irving Stowe, two expat

Americans who had fled to Canada so their sons wouldn't be drafted, and Paul Cote, a Canadian law student. They tried to interest the U.S.-dominated Sierra Club in a protest against American nuclear testing in the Aleutian Islands, but the head office in San Francisco said no.

Thus, by default, the new group started off Canadian, incorporated under the British Columbia Societies Act – a move that turned out to be brilliant. If the committee hadn't started off in this particular country, it would never have evolved into Greenpeace, a powerful organization of international stature. If the Americans had owned it, they'd never have let it go. Ditto for the Brits, French, and Germans, who now dominate Greenpeace. Only Canucks were liberated enough from nationalism to give it away – but that story unfolded long after the first voyage to Amchitka, which none of us imagined would have a sequel, let alone lead to the formation of an eco-navy, complete with a bureaucracy and a political arm, capable (sometimes) of stopping whole megaprojects, fighting such post-space-age nightmares as ozone depletion, genetically modified food, and climate change.

Ninety percent of history is being there, and Vancouver was the only place in the world where a political entity such as Greenpeace could have been born. We had a critical mass of Americans who were really angry with their government. We had the right legal stuff, with sovereignty and anti-piracy rules on our side. We had the biggest concentration of tree-huggers, radicalized students, garbage-dump stoppers, shit-disturbing unionists, freeway fighters, pot smokers and growers, aging Trotskyites, condo killers, farmland savers, fish preservationists, animal rights activists, back-to-the-landers, vegetarians, nudists, Buddhists, and anti-spraying, anti-pollution marchers and picketers in the country, per capita, in the world. If they could be mobilized en masse alongside The Movement's long-haired peacenik hordes – ah, well, we would be talking about a revolution, wouldn't we? John Lennon's *Imagine* played mightily in the background, but Bob Dylan warned: don't follow leaders and watch the parking meters. What was sorely needed was a coherent vision, a philosophy that could embrace them all. From the moment the word "Greenpeace" was first uttered in public, we had it – or we thought we did. Ban the bomb and save the redwoods! Nukes harm trees! At least it was a good start.

Vancouver was the nearest major city to the test zone at Amchitka Island, Alaska, which made it part of the "front line," even if it was protected by Vancouver Island from any tidal waves that might be triggered by the blast. Earthquakes were also a possibility – the fault line leading to San Andreas passed within miles of Amchitka. These dangers spoke to people's very sense of territory. Nowhere else did the general population feel as threatened, and so nowhere else was the story as big. There was a high level of awareness among British Columbians that could be drawn upon like an aquifer, and that sustained Greenpeace through its formative years.

On September 15, 1971, the Don't Make a Wave Committee sent the eighty-foot halibut seiner *Phyllis Cormack*, temporarily renamed the *Greenpeace*, to Amchitka. Twelve men were aboard – John Cormack, the captain; Dave Birmingham, the engineer; and ten eco-freaks ranging in age from twenty-four to fifty-two – and along the way we picked up one more crew member. I have heard our trip described as an odyssey, and so it was, in the modern sense. But in the Homeric sense, it wasn't. The *Odyssey* came later, on the way back from Troy. The story I chronicle here was Greenpeace's *Iliad*.

Cormack was the only skipper on the west coast that the committee could find who was willing to risk his vessel and his life. He brought Birmingham aboard as engineer. The rest of the crew, selected by the committee, were all men – in spite of much talk about New Age-style liberation and equality. This was a sore point, in view of the months of effort that various women had put into raising funds and preparing for the voyage. In fact, the very idea of the trip had been Marie Bohlen's.

The first Greenpeace journey was destined to be every bit as machismo-oriented as the military system it was opposing.

My role on the voyage to Amchitka was that of official chronicler. Not only would I write my regular daily column for *The Vancouver Sun* and transmit each dispatch from the boat by reading it aloud over the radio, I was also expected to write a book about the experience afterwards – if we survived. Another crew member, a young chemistry student named Bob Keziere, was designated the official photographer. Jack McClelland, Canada's most famous publisher, was standing by for the manuscript.

How long ago was 1971? I was still taking notes in longhand, not yet having got around to using a tape recorder. Bob was shooting in black and white. Ben Metcalfe, our senior communications ace, had been provided with a National Film Board 35mm movie camera, but he could barely figure out how to turn it on, let alone deploy it in heavy seas or in the thick of the in-fighting. The bit of fuzzy footage that survives shows us staggering about on a water-slicked deck as the Aleutian Islands and their fang-like rocks heave into view. No sound. At a time when television was taking down American foreign policy in Vietnam, we were fighting with ancient weapons – pencils, notebooks, typewriters, black-and-white photos, and a marine side-band radio that worked mainly at night and only when there was no *Aurora borealis*.

As the ultimate modern theatre of political action, television might as well not have existed. It was like David going into battle with a pea-shooter. I was sensitive to our weakness as a media battleship, having just written a book, *The Storming of the Mind* (McClelland & Stewart, 1971), calling on ecologists to heed Marshall McLuhan's advice: take over the control towers of the mass communications system and deliver new images that will liberate people from their primitive tribal mindsets, creating a new global consciousness. I'd even invented a term: "mind-bombing." My dispatches from the *Greenpeace* were to be a test of my oh-so-hip media theories.

In reality, just getting the columns out was a nightmare. Sometimes I had to shout out the words one letter at a time over the radio to the rewrite guy in the newsroom, and at a crucial juncture, when we got busted, there was no radio contact at all and I had to send my stuff back on a floatplane that flew out only once a week. I fell so far behind in my reportage that the story of the advance of the *Greenpeace* was still running in the papers when we were retreating.

The ultimate literary ignominy lay ahead. When I sat down to write about what had happened, I was in terrible shape. I was chain-smoking and guzzling beer. A back injury I'd suffered in a parachute jump years before was driving me crazy, as it always did when I was stressed, so I was gulping down painkillers and I had to sit with half a dozen pillows strapped around and under me so that my lower spine wouldn't explode as I worked. I couldn't write at home – kids, marital tensions – and forget the office. I'd have to relate to my journalism colleagues at a time when I doubted my own sanity and was completely befuddled by the experience of forty-three days on a boat with eleven other crazies.

In desperation, I retreated to the *Phyllis Cormack*, which was tied up for the winter at the harbour in Steveston, south of Vancouver. Nobody else was aboard, so I could pound my head against the wooden fridge door in the galley and torture myself into telling the story, even though I didn't know yet what had happened to me, or us. History and personal stuff were still mixed up together, and I wasn't documenting so much as groping for the truth. The trip had become a recurring hallucination. Now I had to shake it out of my head word by word, without breaking the train of barely conscious thought, or risk never being able to write it. You either capture it or you don't, and you *know*. I knew, for instance, that everything I was writing through dozens of false starts was shit, even when I had got a dozen pages into it, until the sound of the gulls out on the river flashed me back to the Gulf of Alaska and triggered the flow. Once it was moving, I didn't dare stop. A voice I'd never heard before emerged and truly spoke for me.

Perversely – almost immediately – I developed a duodenal ulcer. My doctor slapped me on a diet of milk and mashed potatoes and said, "Quit writing the book." But he was wrong. I *needed* to write the book. It was pure therapy. Days after the last page passed through my portable Underwood, following a three-week writing binge, the ulcer subsided. I'd written out the story in a single-spaced, one-paragraph, 200-and-some-odd-page stream of consciousness. That was the only way it would come. It was the most sustained, agonizing, ecstatic creative act of my life.

Jack McClelland took one look and shook his Toronto publisher's head. He ordered Keziere and me to reconstitute the project as a photo book with a simple, spare text. We were pros and we dutifully produced it, even though I was smarting to my artistic core, and it made a beautiful, subversive photo book, thanks to Bob's artistry (*Greenpeace*, McClelland and Stewart, 1972). But my poor original angst-ridden prose outburst was axe-dead.

Over the years, as I moved about and worked on other writings, the manuscript got torn apart into segments, some of which got mixed in with other scripts, unfinished novels, essays, word-salad sandwiches, declarations, notes, letters – some archivist may have fun reconstructing it, but my raw reportage effectively disappeared for a generation. I kept meaning to put the story back together but never got around to it. I forgot entirely about the lone photocopy of it that I had laid on Keziere when we worked on the photo book and which, for thirty-two years, remained stuffed in a file among his scrapbooks. Then one fine day in another century, his partner Karen Love came across the copy, like some contemporary Dead Sea scroll, and took it to the editors at Arsenal Pulp Press.

Thus we present a long-forgotten tale from the dawn-time of the New Age. . . .

DURING

A toast as the *Greenpeace* leaves Vancouver. Clockwise from left: Thurston, Metcalfe, Darnell, Cummings, Hunter, Bohlen, Moore, Simmons.

Gulf of Alaska

Gulls yowking, diving, plunging like burst white fragments of a single wing, our wake heaving out behind us gurgling and bubbling, one moment falling down from the stern as though we just soared over a hill, next moment our stomachs being dragged up into a pulpy collision with our lungs and the cold grey boil of the wake wagging over our heads. The boat is rolling like a drum and the horizon is only yards away, coming up like a belch, then dropping out from under, and yet somehow instead of falling we are being pushed into slow, agonizing liftoff, and gravity hauls our stomachs back down like lard into slippery squids of intestine – and then *whack thunk*, as though a boulder had been thrown against the hull, *whoosh*, down we surf in slow-mo into another canyon, and up rears the bow like the head of a dying mastodon, each upward heave a last gasp. *Whack. Thunk.*

We wallow in water suddenly gone still, disengaged from gravity and tides and current, and then we are swing-heaving and lurch-falling again, fumbling through the troughs and clambering to the tops of roaring ocean hills that collapse beneath us. Hiss of water across the old wooden decks, whose brass hatchways to the hold – built for hauls of halibut – are the exact shape of the ecology symbol, the symbol we have on our sail, along with the peace symbol. And the word GREENPEACE,

Northbound.

painted in yellow but now almost impossible to see because the black smoke from the chimney behind the wheelhouse has sooted it out. We poor eco-freaks cringe at the pollution. The engine makes its chugging clunking *snik snik snik snik*, the smoke ghosting out across the sky, white light flaring along the horizon.

Bob Keziere is down in his bunk, face like a squashed grape, long hair sticky with salt, hardly able to talk and certainly not daring to eat. Not that there is much to eat anyway – the cook, Bill Darnell, is collapsed in the bunk above Keziere, face blank, as if involved in some desperate yoga exercise to remove his consciousness from the long yawns and swoop-plunge-lurch-chop takeoffs of the boat and his guts wildly trying to follow. Pat Moore is wedged in between the galley table and the wall, his shoulders pressed back against the wood, feet jammed against the legs of the table, looking like a spaced-out rock star with his frizz of kinky hair and the poster of Richard Nixon above him, Nixon's face blurry and the words: LET ME MAKE MYSELF PERFECTLY CLEAR. Our language has come down to grunts and mutterings, everyone tight-jawed, stiff, sore, bruised from being tossed against walls and bunks. The only way to move is to grab something and haul yourself along hand over hand.

To sleep, I curl up in a fetal ball on my bunk, ass wedged against the guard rail, knees jammed into the wall, both hands gripping the cold pipe that runs through the bunk, expecting any minute to be flipped right out over the edge of it. The dreams are fantastic: my kids on a grassy hill on a windswept plain, my little girl running up and down the slope in utter silence, the grass flattened by a giant invisible foot stalking across the world, my little boy sitting quietly in the arms of a monkey who has long silky hair and a glint of supreme intelligence in her eyes. She is brooding over the boy and watching the girl as she runs. It is a dream of evolution – the children are all alone but for the Wise One from out of the past, an ancestral mother. The world as I know it is gone. The world is lost . . . my children! Ah, but it's a dream, not a vision. It can be explained. Swinging from the rafter over my head is the brown monkey doll my daughter gave me, and the hill and the wind are like the storm and the surging falling sea, and this feeling I have – an urge to sob wildly because my children are out of reach, off in some other world and time, and they will never hear me even if I cry out to them – that can be explained too. *I miss them.*

But there is more. A painful awe opens up inside me. It has been building for days. The sea is the colour of a basilica – granite, limestone, with foam traces of fossil, a hint of archways built of marble – like an immense wrecked cathedral. Standing out on the deck, I have a stoned-out feeling that leaves me tingling and goosebumped, not just from the icy witch-breaths of wind or the terror that this old halibut boat might roll right over and sink. The peace pennants flapping from the rigging, the red and white Canadian flag and the green and gold Greenpeace flag, and above them all, nailed to the top of the mast, the blue and white United Nations flag, all snapping and crackling in the wind. And this old boat – a kind of funky temple, or at least an art object, floundering through the swells. It is incredible that we eco-freaks should be moving out in an assault on the power that put men on the moon, that could blow up the world, in this boat, the *Greenpeace,* in her other life the *Phyllis Cormack.*

She is thirty years old, glossy white with lime trim, with strokes of glistening black along the bumpers of her hull, Rorschach strains of rust running down the enamel like dried blood, and rubber tires dangling from her sides like hippie beads. Her railings, ladders, metal instruments, and huge anchors have been gnawed and sculpted by rust, which is turning green from years of salt water breaking over her decks. The varnish on the wooden walls in the wheelhouse and the john have peeled like films of green skin. She seems a solid piece of wood, this longliner, seiner, fish packer, general anything of a boat,

80 feet long, 102 gross tons, powered by a 17-ton Atlas engine with six cylinders, 230 heavy-duty horsepower and an oil-slicked green mass of machinery, a Disney-animated robot city of pumps and spires and pipes and screaming whirring parts. The noise that blows through the bunks when the hatch to the engine room opens is like an elevated train crashing by. Pipes and fittings and hoses run over the decks, geometric arteries and veins, and the life raft mounted beside the battenclaim is like the one that Captain Ahab rode out in to face down the great white whale. The wheelhouse, which the captain calls the Penthouse, is like the conductor's booth in an old wooden tram. Six wood-frame windows. A night light over the compass bowl with a thick cloth-wrapped wire running down from it like the tube on a hookah. The barometer hangs there, corroded, utterly useless. You have to hammer the depth sounder with your fist to make it work. The mood on the boat is an atmosphere of communion, an aura of High Mass, and far down the long aisle between the rolling sloshing pews stands the skipper, John C. Cormack, a sorcerer alert to invisible presences and forces. The peace and ecology symbols flap on the big green sail above us like hieroglyphs of some weird religion, a whole new Zen-like view of the universe.

Not one of the Don't Make a Wave Committee members on board the *Greenpeace* has set foot in church since he was a kid. Jim Bohlen is a composite materials researcher, space technician, builder of geodesic domes and rocket motors made of filament-wound glass-epoxy resin composites; Pat Moore is a forest biological and interdisciplinary computer simulator man; Terry Simmons is a cultural geographer; Bob Keziere is a chemist and photographer; Bob Cummings writes for the psychedelic mind-blown godless Underground Press; Bill Darnell is a full-time organizer for minority causes; Ben Metcalfe is a theatre critic, journalist, former public relations man; Lyle Thurston is a doctor, about as far into existentialism and phenomenology as you can

Darnell (left) and Cummings in the wheelhouse.

get without being locked up; Dick Fineberg is an associate professor of political science at the University of Alaska. As for myself, I hate churches with a passion, though I will throw the I Ching and admire it as a psychological toy, and generally I agree with Carl Jung's notion of synchronicity.

Yet this protest is somehow connected to the nerve centre where religion dwells, the experience we know as *awe*. The feeling of awe fills the boat, fills our heads and stays there, throbbing gently. Dave Birmingham, the ship's engineer, came into the galley one night shortly after we left Vancouver as we were polishing off the last of the wine someone had donated. We were as raunchy and boozy as guys in a troop train, swearing and singing, and Birmingham said, "I must say I'm disappointed. I'd expected the crew of the *Greenpeace* to be men of religion." Hoots of laughter and catcalls. But now, more than a week later, out in the Gulf of Alaska, with the ocean thrashing around us, a giant across whose flanks we skitter like insects, holding our breath lest the giant roll over in his slumber and crush us, some crust has cracked, some veneer of sophistication has begun to flake away. The first time Moore opened a can of butter upside down, the captain flew into a rage. "Don't you thirty-three-pounders know anything? That's *bad luck!*" And then Darnell hung a coffee cup on a hook facing inward instead of outward, and the captain flipped out again. "That's worse luck! Now you've done it! We're in for it now. . . ." Behind his back, we laughed and shook our heads. Did the old goat really believe that shit? Imagine, a superstitious captain! And yet . . . and yet. . . . Maybe, over the years, sunken boats had been found to have cans in them that were opened upside down, or china cups that faced inward. Maybe it was a pattern – inexplicable, probably coincidental, no doubt meaningless – but. . . .

But now we're out on the Gulf and the swells are coming in 200-foot strides, like a canyon getting up and walking, and, well, when in Rome . . . so we have decided to play it the captain's way. He has been out on these waters for forty years, he tells us, and "There's many a brave heart's gone down to the bottom of the sea." He loves to spoon out sea talk, calling us thirty-three-pounders or mattress-lovers, talking about waves "high as treetops," dismissing the heaving sea as "fuck all" because so far nothing has happened, even though we are already at the point where nobody opens a can upside down and in the morning we all run our eyes nervously over the cups on the hooks. But the awe. That's real – we all feel it.

In less than a week, if everything goes well, we will be within three miles of Amchitka Island, where the Americans will blast off an underground hydrogen bomb 250 times as powerful as the artificial sun that burned over Hiroshima. It might leak radiation. It might trigger an earthquake. It might set a tidal wave in motion. We will be at the gates of hell, it is as simple as that. Maybe we will wave our microphones and cameras and notebooks like crucifixes at the gate, but our tape recorder and marine side-band radio and cameras and other electronic wands, and the hieroglyphs on our sail and the peace pennants flapping from the rigging, are finally not much protection against radiation and shock waves. Moore brought along a Geiger counter, so at least we will know if the decks are being swept by Strontium-90 or Cesium-136 and we can try to make a run for it. The guys who have already had kids – Metcalfe, Bohlen, Birmingham, and I – will go out on deck in slicks and gumboots and try to wash down the walls, while the other guys hole up in the engine room, trying to keep their genes out of reach of the invisible poisons.

The Bomb itself is awesome. When it is triggered, pressure in the firing chamber will rise to more than a hundred million pounds per square inch in about one-millionth of a second, and the temperature will leap to about a hundred million degrees Fahrenheit, instantly vapourizing hundreds of thousands of tons of solid rock, creating a spherical gas-filled chamber in the earth like a giant glazed light bulb. We will be sitting at the edge of the three-mile territorial limit of Amchitka, and the bomb will go off about a mile inland. All ships within fifty miles of the island will have been warned away. The only other human beings in that area will be a group of U.S. Atomic Energy Commission technicians locked up in a concrete bunker mounted on steel springs twenty miles from the test site at the other end of the island, behind a mountain range. The risk? Out of eighty-three underground tests in Nevada, triggered at depths greater than 300 feet, seven tests leaked, so the chances are at least eight out of a hundred. But Nevada is a relatively stable geological area. By contrast, the Aleutian Islands have been described by one geographer as "the scene of some of the freakiest geological happenings on the planet," where earthquakes strike several times a week and volcanoes are still active. No one knows how much greater that makes the chance of radiation leakage

Two previous tests have been done at Amchitka: a "small" eighty-kiloton blast in 1964 – conducted in secret – and a one-megaton blast in 1969. The first explosion, code-named Longshot, leaked. The second, Milrow, did not. It is a small sample, but the leakage record for tests on the island is one hit, one miss. This third blast will be five times as large as Milrow. It will be called Cannikin, which sounds like something out of the worst early 1950s science fiction pulp magazines – a beast name, like a monster in *Lord of the Rings*, an atomic fire-breathing dragon. This is the mythical overtone. We are like Bilbo Baggins and the dwarves attempting to get to the lair of Smaug. No – more like the Fellowship of the Ring – the Ring of Power, which for us is the closed-circle ecology symbol – and we are on our way to the dread dark land of Mordor, and Amchitka is Mount Doom, and Cannikin is the very Crack of Doom. Somehow we have to hurl the Ring of Power into the fire and bring down the whole kingdom of the Dark Lord, whose blurred face looks out from the poster in the galley. We are the Fellowship of the Piston Rings. And if there is a sorcerer aboard, a Gandalf the Grey, it is

Thurston on deck.

Captain John Cormack, for he is the only one with the magic knowledge that will get us across the ocean and through whatever perilous passes and storms we will run into along the way.

To the rest of us, who have almost no practical experience with the sea, the ocean itself is mythical territory. Moore opens another can upside down and we all pounce and throw the cursed thing overboard. Then fall into giggling fits, we space technicians and hard-nosed journalists, academics, and political radicals, floundering in confusion as we try to grasp new responses appropriate to this weird scene. We should have brought the I Ching. We should have brought a lot of things. But it's too late now. *The awe. . . .*

Not just the wonder and vastness of the open sea, but the screwy things that have been happening all the way. Like the synchs Tom Wolfe talks about in *The Electric Kool-Aid Acid Test.* The synchs happen with mysterious regularity, pieces falling together naturally, forces slipping into play, combinations of events and people so perfect, so beautiful, so weird and unlikely that it rocks our heads, it loosens the old logic, it drives us deeper into the growing sense of awe and magic, the sense that we are part of a vast unfolding pattern of events.

When the journalists among us – Metcalfe, Keziere, and I – attacked the Amchitka plan in print, we had freely used the phrase "nuclear John Wayneism." One of my pieces, which was read into the Congressional Record in the U.S.A., said that Amchitka might be the Custer's Last Stand of the weapons-makers. And then, on the very day we pulled out of Vancouver – September 15, 1971 – who pulled in at Victoria, just across the Strait of Georgia, in his converted minesweeper? *John Wayne,* the reincarnation of mad George Custer himself. Asked about our protest voyage to Amchitka, the arch-cowboy growled, "They're a bunch of Commies." It was perfect. Canadians should "mind their own business," he said With B.C. right in the path of any radiation leaking from Amchitka, right in the path of any tidal wave that might sweep across the Pacific, Wayne's statement wiped out any remaining public opposition to our protest. Even local ultra-conservatives were suddenly yelling, "Yankee go home!" and cheering us on.

And then, two days out of Vancouver, heading up through Johnstone Strait around the northeast tip of Vancouver Island, we got a radio message from the town of Alert Bay, asking us to stop in. A group of people came down to the dock and gave us a couple of fresh coho salmon. Two Kwak'waka'wakw women, Lucy and Daisy Sewid, came aboard to give us the support of all the aboriginal people on the west coast. They invited us to stop in on the way back and carve our names on a totem pole they were carving, which would be the tallest one in the world. The arch-cowboy was against us and the Indians were on our side.

I had brought along a book called *Warriors of the Rainbow*, a collection of Native legends and prophecies. In it was a core legend that predicted a time when the Natives would be almost completely wiped out by the white man, and the forests would be chopped down and the water and the skies poisoned. At that time the Natives would rediscover their spirits and teach the white man how to live in the world without wrecking it. They would become Warriors of the Rainbow. Thus baptized by the Kwak'waka'wakws, we headed on up the coast, shaking our heads and laughing at the perfect coincidence. Some time later, Chief Dan George, the only Native North American ever to come within arm's reach of an Oscar, spoke out publicly against the test. Chief Dan was one of Lyle Thurston's patients, and when Thurston heard the news, he lay back in his bunk and chuckled and chortled, muttering over and over again, "Unreal! Unreal! Absolutely unreal, man!" John Wayne and the U.S. Atomic Energy Commission vs. Chief Dan George and the Warriors of the Rainbow.

Down in the bunkroom – which we renamed the Opium Den because the ten bunks are stacked in twos in a space the size of a bathroom – someone has tacked up posters of a magnificent ancient blue frigate, ornate as a gingerbread house. Its name is *Friendship Frigate*, and the sunset into which it sails is pure psychedelic – golden flows of lava and a giant popcorn cloud white as the gulls spilling down around its sails. Down through a cosmos of the blown mind the frigate rides into new eras and new depths of being, a flagship of the Aquarian Age. On its sail, delicate as the pattern on a butterfly wing, is the peace symbol. With that and the ecology symbol, we are one step farther out than *Friendship Frigate*.

Up the Inside Passage along the west coast we have chugged, flagship of the new consciousness, the Warriors of the Rainbow attacking a nuclear Little Big Horn, with the prayers of the Indians behind us, plowing smoothly through a great technicolor eruption of Beautiful British Columbia postcards, the sweetest Indian summer on the coast in years, the sun sending three-dimensional spots of pure light down on the beer commercial blue waters, mountain slopes rising like perfect Zen states above walls of forest surrounding the boat, rocks drifting by with seams like ancient faces – and down through the narrow passages blew thousands and millions of seeds, each large enough to be an angel insect dancing above the water, glinting like snowflakes against the purple shadows. North through the Strait of Georgia, into Discovery Passage, over the hump of Vancouver Island, through a maze of channels and inlets and sounds and bays and passes and rivers and creeks, up along Johnstone Strait into the wide island-littered mouth of Queen Charlotte Sound, and immediately the motion of the boat changed from slow caboose to long glides of flow and rise, ripples transformed into great booms of rolling water. Then, as suddenly as they had come, the swells were gone, and we were in the shelter of Calvert Island and moving up Fitz Hugh Sound, turning west at Denny Island, through the tight narrow channel of Lamas Passage, winding northward again past Bella Coola, then west out to Milbanke

The crew of the *Greenpeace*, photographed by crew-member Keziere. Clockwise from top left: Hunter, Moore, Cummings, Metcalfe, Birmingham, Cormack, Darnell, Simmons, Bohlen, Thurston, Fineberg.

Sound, north into Finlayson Channel, up the long bow of Princess Royal Channel into Wright Sound – a nexus of disintegrating jigsaw puzzle pieces of island, and up the avenue of Grenville Channel, out into Dixon Entrance. Now the faint silver veins of the mountains are engulfed by the swells, and our last glimpse of the continent is a line of rubble, early winter dusk rising like smoke, cold breaths of sea witches fogging the portholes and chilling the decks, sunset a flare of white in the puddles and foam on the poop deck, billows of cloud with traces of dark brass.

It was never our intention to go to Amchitka and park there through Zero Hour to protest against war. We are eco-freaks, arguing that the world itself was being destroyed. Even without war, we are doomed. Even if the nuclear button is never pressed, within fifty or sixty years we will pass the point of no return and planet Earth will no longer be fit for human life. Cannikin is as much a monster of pollution as of war machinery, and it is the spectre of a dead world that haunts us, that drove us out against the Cold Warriors in this funky old boat.

As it turns out, the northern B.C. coast cannot have been a more perfect place to pass through on our way to Amchitka. It is already the graveyard for a civilization that was devastated by disease, and another that is in the process of decay. Abandoned canneries stand along the shores – patchworks of warehouses made of rusting corrugated sheet metal, broken windows, sheds perched on barnacled pilings, wood collapsed as though burned and swathed in gauze, bull kelp floating among the sagging wharves, jellyfish drifting in the silence. Streams leak down into tiny deltas that gurgle across moon-beds of tideflats, past the wrecks of old fishing boats. Under the impact of technology, the herring population has been dying off. Now the halibut are dwindling and whales are rare. One by one the canneries have been closing down, and as the fish died off, the government stopped issuing fishing licences and cut down on the number of fishermen. The white men devastated the land and then retreated, leaving the Natives to live among the derelict canneries and boats along the beaches. In the *Greenpeace* we chugged up past stretches of coastline whose deathly silence was like a forewarning of what was to come – the West has already begun its great fall.

Set back in the lush, cool forest, where we couldn't see them, stood hundreds of petrified creatures, symbols of an earlier devastation, the attack on the magnificent civilizations of the Coast Salish, the Nuu-chah-nulth, Kwak'waka'wakw, Bella Coola, Haida, and Tsimshian. No new totem poles or housefronts had joined the aging ones standing like death masks, the skulls splintered and the huge eyes staring out as though hypnotized, tall gods thrown down in a slow green explosion. Some vibration lay tingling on the water, a mood of awe. Another synch – on our way to try to prevent a blow to our own civilization, we pass through the land of one that barely survived its own terrible blow. *Destruction happens.* Whole civilizations die. There is almost a buzz in the air.

On Sunday, four days out of Vancouver, we were up in the Penthouse and Thurston reverently stacked two stereo cassettes in the wooden tray in front of the wheel – Beethoven's Fifth and a Moody Blues album, *On the Threshold of a Dream.* We were all bruised and numb from the batterings of the last few days, groggy from anti-seasickness pills, and the music of the Moody Blues rises from the tape recorder like a flock of birds.

> Tell us what you've seen
> In faraway forgotten lands
> Where empires have turned back to sand.

Well, we had seen abandoned canneries and old wrecked fishing boats, and we had picked up a mysterious psychic buzz emanating from the staggered totem poles, and we had seen that fish and whales were dying off and that immense tracts of forest along the coast had been stripped bare. The steering wheel was a torture rack at first, like trying to guide a herd of elephants with one thin rein, and the boat zigzagged slowly for the first few days, swinging one way, then the other, each of us grunting and grappling furiously with the wheel, trying to keep her on course. But the wheel evolved into a mandala, and the chain that clattered and rattled through the first few nights as we swung her wildly this way and that was clinking now like the bracelets of a Tibetan princess.

Sweeps of clouds and light. Triumphs of music moving through the Penthouse as solemnly as the sea. Now not only were we being borne along like a tram, we were being swept by electric swells, rocked in long pendulum-swings of sound. The sunset was the colour of a cataract, but now the light moved up the spectrum only to the lower hues of brass, which matched exactly the mood of the music. Lyrics came through between plunges and wallowings of the boat.

It all unfolds before your eyes.

The music was full of the crashing of cymbals and deeps of a piano. It plunged, it rose, harpsichord passages trailed out like thin wires, organ swells advanced from out in the silence, drumbeats were lured into its orbit, concertos were mustered like storms. It trickled, rained, flowed down through our heads, pianos surfacing like whales, racing toward us with twitching keyboards.

Now you know how nice it feels.

Thurston swayed in the movement of the boat, eyes closed, music crashing down through his mind, toppling him into realms beyond the reach of words. He was humming and conducting the orchestra, which was like calling forth the waves and pulling the clouds across the sky and making the boat surge and pause as it groped through the swells. Everything was in motion, inside Thurston's head and out. The boundaries had all dissolved. He was back in oceanic consciousness. Thurston, born in Saskatchewan, was perfect material for a sailor – no fear of wide open spaces. No fear, period, as far as I could see, although he did mention that being the ship's doctor was the best job on a boat until something went wrong, and then it was the worst. The music soared through the Penthouse and echoed down into the Opium Den, luring the other crew members. Moore climbed up through the hatchway. Fineberg wedged himself between the radar and the door. Darnell shed enough seasickness to join us, wearing an engineer's cap, a string of beads, and flaming yellow suspenders. Keziere groped his way up out of his bunk, still sick and weak, but grooving on the meshings of music and sea motion. Thurston went on conducting the orchestra while I took my turn at the wheel, Cummings puffed on a pipe, and Simmons slouched under the depth sounder, chin bursting with the first prickles of red beard, hands disappearing into the pockets of his blue nylon jacket as though amputated. We all swayed with the *Greenpeace* and the Moody Blues, jammed together like commuters on a train, saying nothing, just humming along, riding up and up and up to white sky and grey sea and dark varnish-peeling wood and pale wasted faces, down down down toward the bottom of a wide sea valley with a canyon of water marching toward us.

Then the radio room door opened and Bohlen hauled himself into the packed Penthouse, coughing from all the cigarette smoke. "Well," he said, "the Fabulous Furry Freak Brothers." He was right – that's exactly what we looked like, only shaggier and shabbier and more wasted.

He pointed at the tape recorder right beside the compass. "Hey, isn't that going to throw the magnet off?"

"Nah," somebody reassured him.

"Are you sure?"

"Sure."

Actually we weren't sure, but the scene was so delightful, nobody wanted to mess it up.

In fact, the tape recorder *did* affect the compass. While we were grooving on the Moody Blues, the *Greenpeace* wandered ninety miles off course. It was no sweat off our noses – we were well ahead of schedule, at least eleven days to go before Cannikin was expected to go off. But our accidental side trip cost the American taxpayers something like $22,000.

We made no effort to cover our tracks. Metcalfe regularly radioed our position and course to his wife Dorothy. And Dorothy got a request from the Coast Guard commander in Juneau to keep them "posted" – just in case we got in trouble. Wouldn't want the boys to run into bad weather and not be able to find them. Sure, sure. So on Monday, the day after the Moody Blues sent us off course, a notice went up on the flight schedule board at Kodiak: SEARCH CAN VES GREEN PEACE, and the 17th District of the U.S. Coast Guard, armed with specific data about our speed, position, and course, dispatched a Navy plane, a Hercules HC-130 from Kodiak, Alaska, to run out over the Gulf and get some pictures of us for identification purposes later on. The tab on one hour of flying time for a Hercules was $1,100, and they spent ten hours tracking us because the CAN VES GREEN PEACE wasn't where it was supposed to be.

Late Monday night the Hercules swung back into Kodiak, not having found a trace of its prey. At the headquarters of the 17th District, the only conclusion to draw was that we had deliberately deceived the Coast Guard, that we were sneaky bastards, and that if we could elude them on the open seas in our thirty-year-old fishing boat that does no more than nine knots at full throttle, what tricks must we have up our

Aircraft surveillance by a U.S. Navy plane dispatched from Kodiak, Alaska.

sleeves for later, when we got close to Amchitka?

Yesterday morning the notice went back up on the flight board: SEARCH CAN VES GREEN PEACE. And the Hercules came gliding across the waves at us like a silver steel albatross on the hunt, four long fingers of smoke trailing from its wings, sound mounting from a hiss to a whine to a mutter, a moan, a howl, *huuuuuuuuuuuu,* down to a wail, a rumble, a faraway wind. Then out and out it headed in the opposite direction. It banked and took another run, like a strafing run, except that the side door was open and they were shooting us with their cameras. Keziere fired back with his Leica, and Metcalfe trundled out the sleek Japanese 15mm movie camera loaned to us by the National Film Board. They took pictures of us for the record and we took pictures of them for the record, and it was a war between two motion picture studios making two completely different movies with completely different bad guys. It was a McLuhan-type war, a war of the icons, a public relations struggle.

In addition to the $22,000 we estimate the Coast Guard spent finding us and photographing us, the Atomic Energy Commission is going to have to spend plenty on public relations to patch up the damage. We have planned for a high level of exposure in the mass media. The only way we can make any impact is to keep ourselves in the spotlight the whole time. That's why we emphasized media when we selected the crew. Metcalfe would handle public relations. He'd send reports every night to Dorothy, who would immediately dispatch them to radio, TV, newspapers, and wire services. Cummings would file his stuff with Vancouver's underground paper, *The Georgia Straight,* which would pass it on to all the underground papers in Canada, the U.S., and Europe via the Liberation News Service. I would pump out a daily column to *The Vancouver Sun.* Fineberg would get stories out to papers in Alaska and to a small radical wire service called Dispatch International, based in Washington, D.C.

With the delivery of this information to the media as our sling, we will hurl our stone – the *Greenpeace* – against the American Goliath. Our boat is to be a tiny domino that we will push so that it falls against the larger domino of public opinion in Vancouver. That larger domino will topple the giant domino of public opinion right across Canada, and that giant piece might fall hard enough to knock down the super-pyramid of public opinion in the United States. The last decade of turmoil in the U.S. fused the Civil Rights movement with the anti-war movement, which had its roots in Ban the Bomb, a worldwide campaign that started in Great Britain in the 1950s. Civil Rights demonstrations and peace marches made the walls tremble. Now, virtually overnight, a vast environmental movement has come into being, born out of a sudden awareness that the planet itself is being destroyed. We need to pull this trinity of changes together, fusing the clenched fist and the broken cross and the closed circle of unity. Here, with the notion of Greenpeace, is an alliance that might finally wrest the Cold Warriors out of the control tower. In these times, what larger ambition can be dreamed? It is as monumental a quest as for the Ring of Power.

But power corrupts. Each of us runs the risk of being corroded, like the Bearer of the Ring. Just when Frodo the Hobbit finally reaches the Crack of Doom and is ready to hurl the Ring into the fire to bring down the kingdom of the Dark Lord, the poor guy finds that he can't let go of the Ring. Its power has corrupted him, taking over his soul.

Metcalfe sensed early in the voyage that we might be in for some heavy shocks and trials, and he gave us two warnings. First, "Fear success." Second, "Beware of paranoid grandiosity." Here's the *Encyclopaedia Britannica* definition: "Paranoid grandiosity tends to be well organized, relatively stable and persistent. The complexity of delusional conviction varies from rather simple beliefs in one's alleged talent, attractiveness or inspiration to highly complex, systematized beliefs that one is a great prophet, author, poet, inventor or scientist. The latter extreme belongs to classical paranoia." Well, the *Greenpeace*, suffused with our grand ambition to cripple the Megamachine of the nuclear weapons makers, is a floating paranoid grandiosity trap. The ambition gets into our heads, tricking us into thinking we are a hundred or ten thousand times as important as we are, and this can warp our perception of reality. Careful, careful. Tread gingerly along the wire, boys! We have to keep talking each other down from bad paranoid grandiosity trips. Remember, we're just a dozen middle-class cats out here on an old boat, away from our warm, comfortable Canadian Hobbit holes. All we can hope to do is concentrate public attention on the test at Amchitka, to provide a focal point for opposition – which is growing all the time. All we'll be doing is what millions of other people have already done – establish a picket line, a floating picket line.

But the trap is slippery with quicksilver. Just before we reached the open sea, the Prime Minister of Canada tried to raise us on the radiophone. He couldn't get through, but he did issue a statement opposing the test. It was a major political victory – and the beginning of a transformation. In its final edition on Monday, the day the Hercules went out looking for us, *The Vancouver Sun* ran a full eight-column headline: TRUDEAU CONDEMNS TEST AT AMCHITKA, followed by an article that Dorothy Metcalfe read to us triumphantly over the radio:

> Prime Minister Pierre Elliott Trudeau issued a statement
> Sunday condemning the proposed Amchitka nuclear test –
> but he failed to get the message to the crew members of the
> Greenpeace protest vessel. A spokesman for Greenpeace
> said in Vancouver that Trudeau tried to contact the crew
> via radio, but the ship was in the Grenville Channel near
> Prince Rupert and out of radio contact. She is sailing
> towards Amchitka Island off Alaska in an attempt to halt
> the nuclear test schedule by the United States government

for sometime during the next few weeks. Trudeau's statement notes his "great concern for an issue which is causing anxiety to Canadians generally and so very much more so to the citizens of B.C." The statement continues: "The proposed underground nuclear testing at Amchitka has been the subject of numerous consultations between the Canadians and U.S. governments. The Canadian government has informed the United States administration that it cannot agree with the proposed testing and that we believe all such tests should be halted. . . ." Meanwhile, a protest telegram containing 6,000 names was sent to U.S. President Richard Nixon Sunday night by the Canadian Coalition To Stop The Amchitka Bomb.

Well, hurray hurray! It had been a long time since a protest got the backing of a head of state. We cheered – a bit. It was a wishy-washy statement, and when you boiled it down and examined the remains, it was pure cabbage talk. Trudeau merely acknowledged that there was a lot of public feeling against the test. Norman Mailer observed: "In a modern state, the forces of propaganda control leaders as well as citizens, because the forces of propaganda are more complex than the leaders." But hold on. Nobody thinks for a moment that we can do a single thing to halt the test, unless the Atomic Energy Commission is far more worried about radiation leakage than they admit. If so, they will have to find some way to bust us or kick us out of the area, because if it does leak, and that Geiger counter of Moore's starts clicking away, we'll be on the radio getting the news back as fast as we can. And if we get sprayed with radiation, the Atomic Energy Commission will be stuck with a dozen martyrs on its hands, and maybe they don't like that idea. But halt the test? Careful, now! Fear success, boys! It's true that right from the day Bohlen announced to the press that a ship would be going to Amchitka, the word "blockade" had been bandied about. Some serious arguments were even put forward to the effect that the *Greenpeace* may be the straw that breaks the Megamachine's back. *If* enough political pressure can be brought to bear, *if* the issue fires up enough people, *if* we draw enough attention to the island, then our presence offshore might be enough to tip the scales.

At the same time, there is a weird absence of ego in the protest. The United States can blow up the world if it wants. Can we really pretend to ourselves that we can throw the Cold Warriors to the floor? Maybe we are too modest, too rational. Maybe we need more ego, not less. Enough ego to imagine that we can throw down the empire. The energy that motivates us, that built up the venture and sustained it through amazing transformations, is generated by the urge to stop the bastards. Yet here we are, at the very speartip of the attack, trying to stay cool, to keep our perspective. The call from Trudeau had the effect of making us the unofficial official Canadian Navy, and now the media are watching us like hawks. If the paranoia level twitched upward at the U.S. Coast Guard when their Hercules failed to find us, it was nothing compared to the convulsion of paranoid grandiosity that shuddered through the *Greenpeace* when we found out that the Prime Minister picked up the phone. Now we had all of Canada behind us.

The pictures that the Yanks took from the Hercules would have shown them clearly that in addition to the life raft near the stern and the two inflatable rafts up behind the Penthouse, there is an aluminum skiff and an outboard motor lying out on the poop deck. In fact, we have seriously discussed the possibility of three or four of us leaping into the skiff at the last minute and making a run for the island. We know that Captain John will not enter the three-mile territorial limit. If he does, his vessel can be confiscated, and each of us is subject to a $10,000 fine and ten years in jail. He will be powerless to stop us from jumping into the skiff in the last hours before the bomb goes off

Thurston in his bunk, writing.

and racing across the water to make a landing on the island. That is, if anybody is willing to do it. The question is open. Each of us will have to make his own decision. At first I guessed that Bohlen and Moore might try it. They strike me as the most radical of the bunch. Will I join them? Well, goddamn, it is going to be an exquisite moment of torture. The mirror will flare to unbearable intensity and there, stark naked and absolutely visible, will be the revelation of each of our essential inner selves, too vivid for any of us ever again to pretend to strength, passion, or conviction that we do not have.

It is not the thought of certain death that hangs me up, it is the thought of rotting in jail for ten years. It is hard enough to go through the agony of deciding to go on the damn boat in the first place. Life is sweet in these years on the west coast of Canada, and though the Golden Age is near its end, storms of environmental ruin lie ahead, the oceans will die, the whales and fish will disappear, the land will be poisoned, and the cities will become rat traps of rape and murder and mayhem as they are already becoming in America, and though soon enough radiation will begin to leak from all those places where it is trapped underground or in lead-lined tanks, and though the world will be a gas chamber and a sink hole and millions of people will be killed by famines and plagues – though all of this comes down on our heads like an avalanche, life is still sweet on the west coast. Canada is like the Shire where the peace-loving Hobbits live, sucking on their pipes and eating six times a day, and I don't want to leave it, leave my wife and kids and good friends and cozy Establishment job. Shit, no.

The other guys on the boat, including Bob Cummings, who is supposed to be our ambassador from the Land of Counterculture, live lives no less sweet. Doc Thurston is, well, a doctor, Moore and Keziere and Simmons work for Establishment universities, Metcalfe for the Establishment Canadian Broadcasting Corporation, Bohlen for the Establishment Government of Canada. Birmingham owns a hunk of land on Vancouver Island and the skipper belongs to the Shipowners Association, the capitalists of the fishing industry, even if he is very much a working-class hero who worked his way up from a deckhand job. Even Darnell, an organizer of minority and environment causes, works for the Company of Young Canadians, a government-funded make-work program that is about as revolutionary as the Boy Scouts. We all live sweet lives, we are part of an aristocracy, so it is doubly hard for us to get our asses moving. We decided that something had to be done, that it wasn't enough just to write and talk about it, that we needed a real life-or-death engagement. To have gone through all of that and to arrive at a point where we are actually floundering across the Gulf of Alaska, with storms lying up ahead and dangerous passes to manoeuvre in a boat that a number of fishermen told us is too broken-down to get us through, on our way toward the very gates of twentieth-century hell – well, it changed us. It was a tremendous relief finally to be in motion, finally to have joined the army, to be on our way to a battlefield in a war that has to be waged if the tailspin of pollution and war is ever to be halted. A revolution is in the works – nothing less will turn the tide – and once you have joined the Revolution, brothers and sisters, you are smack at the doorway leading into the Temple of Paranoid Grandiosity.

And meanwhile, our tender asses are smarting. Life has become distinctly uncomfortable. Thurston's porthole leaks and icy water keeps splashing over his feet, while his head is wedged against the wall containing the chimney that runs up from the engine room, which is usually about 120 degrees Fahrenheit, and the thunder of the great Atlas blasts continually from below, and a transom in the floor of the radio room directly above the Opium Den lets through all the LSD shrieks and whistles coming out of the radio at night when Metcalfe or Cummings or I try to get our reports through storms of static to Vancouver (the radio doesn't work during the day because of all the electromagnetic convulsions lying between us and the shore). What sounds! From the radio comes the noise of a torture chamber, or a lizard being hatched at the dawn of time, screeches and squawks and wild whimpering gurgles. All of this as we try to sleep, while the sound from the engine below – well, a power lawn mower would be a hum in comparison. Explosions of gasoline and air rubbing, clanking, vibrating, spent gases detonating, the fan belt screaming for help, explosions within explosions, cylinders and pistons pounding. Then there's the clattering and crashing of pots and pans all night long, china dishes smashing on the galley floor, and the weird noises of the sea. *What was that?* Sounds like . . . like . . . would you believe two giant squids copulating? An enormous underwater bat rubbing its leathery wings against the hull? A human skeleton rattling around in a big tin box? A huge wet kiss being planted on the porthole from outside? Easy to understand where myths and legends about sea monsters come from. You could freak out at night, lying in your bunk, sure that you heard the *slap flap flop* of a monster from the Black Lagoon walking around on the decks. No chance of sleeping, not with all those noises and the boat still doing its drum-roll acrobatics, great sudden thumps as though – I swear – a boulder has just hit the hull.

And then there's the problem of having amateurs at the wheel. One night Metcalfe is half asleep on duty in the Penthouse – a sensory deprivation chamber at night, since Cormack insists on no light except for the tiny bulb over the compass, "otherwise you can't see a damn thing outside." (But John, I can't see a damn thing anyway. "Goddamn weak-eyed landlubbers can't even see at night!") – and he gets caught unawares by an enormous wave. A sudden lurch, sudden kamikaze leaps of chinaware from the shelves in the galley, exploding like grenades, *clatter whang ching* of frying pans and kettles and tin cups, and the boat takes a sickening sideways plunge like a buffalo that's been shot. Metcalfe is thrown down but hangs onto the wheel, whirling the whole boat around, and by the time he can get to his feet and stop the mad spin of the wheel, the boat, which was going due west, is suddenly going due east, and four or five of us have been thrown out of our bunks. Up in the radio room, above the skipper, the wooden guard rail on Fineberg's bunk breaks when his body is hurled against it, and he sails through the air and lands with a horrible thud. To the rest of us down below, it sounds like the whole Penthouse is splitting and breaking off. Splash and whack of waves snapping against my porthole like wet towels. God, we're going down! "Oh, fuck around," yells Thurston. "Shape up, Metcalfe, or you're fired! Goddamn, what'm I doing here!" Moore: "Isn't it awful?" Darnell: "Bhleeeee." Keziere: "Yuks." He has barely begun to get over his seasickness, and now his stomach is collapsing back into the stew pots. Moving like a man half paralyzed, he gets up and gropes his way to the galley and out the door to puke. No sooner has he pushed open the door than a vast screaming silver and black amoeba of water hits the deck like a thousand sheets of plate glass, soaking him and almost washing him away. "Fuck's sake," he mutters, "a guy can't even have a decent puke around here."

Somebody starts whistling "We Love You, Greenpeace" – our theme song. We picked it up at Klemtu, the Kitasoo fishing village in Finlayson Channel, 355 miles up the coast from Vancouver. We'd put in there so Cormack could do some welding on a boiler plate, way back in the days when we were chugging up the Inside Passage. My, doesn't that seem a long time ago, even though we have only been out on the open sea for three or four days – or is it five? The Kitasoo kids had converged on the old rotting wharf where we were moored (symbolic abandoned cannery looming behind them), excited because Keziere and Moore and Thurston and I looked like real hippies, and white society has never produced a figure so loved by Native children as the hippie. "Wow, they look just like us!" It could even be argued that the appearance of the hippie signalled the beginning of the great reversal in white Western society, what with the grandchildren of the cowboys turning out to be more like Indians than spacemen. The only link these kids have with the weird futuristic supercivilization a couple of hundred miles down the coast – as far out of reach as the moon for most of them – is television, and on television they had watched the *Greenpeace* depart from Vancouver. And here we were, the first television image that had ever come to life in front of them. They swarmed over the decks and hung around for the whole five or six hours we were there.

We walked through the village and rapped with anyone who could talk to us, then slunk back to the boat, guilty and depressed because of the bum deal the Indians were getting, how badly they'd been ripped off by us white people. Now the kids wanted us to come out on deck and perform whatever magic tricks we had done to get ourselves on television. As a matter of fact, we put on a not-bad show. They sang songs and Metcalfe swung out on the upper deck with his tape recorder. The rest of us straggled out on the deck, one by one, in a much better mood, having finished off a couple of bottles of wine and the last of the salmon we'd been given at Alert Bay. The kids went through a bunch of nursery rhymes and the national anthem, to which Keziere responded, "Can't you do better than that, you kids?" and then they struck up a catchy tune, "We Love You, Conrad," from the Broadway musical *Bye Bye Birdie*. After a couple of rounds, the kids started yelling at us to tell them our names. One by one Metcalfe shouted out our names, and one by one the kids sang:

> We love you, Uncle Ben,
> Oh yes we do,
> We love you, Uncle Ben (or Bob or Bill or Dave or Pat or Lyle),
> And we'll be true,
> When you're not near to us, we're blue,
> Oh Uncle Ben, we love you.

The vibes were terrific. Then Darnell shouted, "What do you think of Greenpeace?" And the kids, with us singing along as loud as we could, burst into a beautiful full-throated passionate rendition:

> We love you, Greenpeace,
> Oh yes we do,
> We love you, Greenpeace,
> And we'll be true. . . .

And as the boat chugged away into the darkness, the kids were still singing, "Oh Greenpeace, we love you," and tearing off their headbands and plastic peace symbols and rings made of beads and throwing them at us and cheering and yelling and whooping, and we were all gathered out on the stern, singing back at them, "We love you, Klemtu!" Damn if Bohlen and I weren't almost crying by the time it was over.

Since then, whenever things get rough, somebody starts singing or humming "We Love You, Greenpeace" as an anthem, a gentle reminder that it's a good cause, and let's not blow our cool. Like now, the boat having swung around 180 degrees while Metcalfe crashed to the floor of the Penthouse, Fineberg crashed to the floor of the radio room, pots and pans and china dishes crash everywhere, and the squid-ink darkness envelops us, waves breaking across the decks, most of us convinced in our half-asleep stupor that the old boat has finally given up the ghost and we are on our way down to Davy Jones' locker – now we all start singing "We Love You, Greenpeace" between fits of swearing and complaining. Only a couple more weeks, guys, then it'll all be over and – touchy touchy wood – we'll all be safe and sound back in our little Hobbit holes and puffing on our pipes and telling fantastic stories about the fire-breathing dragon and the dread land of Mordor and how Captain Cormack's Lonely Hearts Club Band went out to save the world by. . . .

"Did you say a couple of *weeks?*" moans Cummings from directly below me. "Aaaaarrrghhh!" Poor Cummings. A year ago – no, longer than that, two years ago – he was described in *The Rolling Stone* as being "close to the breaking point." As managing editor of *The Georgia Straight*, he had been busted repeatedly. The *Straight* – acknowledged as the most harassed and hassled underground paper in North America – faced so many charges at one point that the editor stood to go to jail for a total of seventeen years. The strain had got to Cummings. He had finally resigned as managing editor and spent the summer recuperating in Mexico. But now he is getting that harassed look again.

Then the blow lands. Moore and Darnell and I are down in the galley when the skipper comes tromping in from the poop deck and says, "Test's been delayed." *Wham.* We let out three simultaneous groans. We are eight days out of Vancouver and within one day's sailing of the Aleutians, and from there it is only a matter of 400 miles to Amchitka. The delay, according to the newspapers, will set the test back until at least early November. The effect on us is something like what an astronaut might feel if he was descending in his module toward the surface of the moon, and the moon suddenly leapt fifty billion miles away.

We convene a meeting in the galley, which at this moment becomes the boardroom of Greenpeace Inc. There are several questions with no answers attached. Is the report accurate? Is it a trick cooked up by the Atomic Energy Commission to throw us off the track? Or is that pure paranoid grandiosity? The thing is, we don't have the faintest idea whether the *Greenpeace* matters or not. It may be that by parking so close to the blast, we are creating a bad political situation for the weapons freaks. Canadian-American relations are at a low point because of a number of otherwise unrelated factors, like trade issues and the Vietnam war and dealings with China. Inevitably, the opposition building up against the test back home is taking on anti-American

Captain Cormack (right) and engineer Birmingham.

overtones. Even U.S. congressmen and senators are mumbling about how awful it will be if America's critical alliances with Canada get too badly strained, Canada having become America's last great stash of natural resources after they trashed their own. It will not do to have a Canadian boat and crew wiped out at Amchitka, especially a boat with such broad public support that the Prime Minister himself had to endorse the protest. But it isn't likely that the test has been delayed just to shake us off. Premier Kosygin of Russia is due to arrive in Canada soon for a cross-country tour, and it will be bad diplomacy to blow the bomb while he is on tour. Emperor Hirohito will arrive in Alaska not long after that, and Nixon will be coming up to shake his hand, and it will be even worse diplomacy to blow the bomb virtually under the Emperor's ass, especially since America's alliance with Japan is strained as badly as their alliance with Canada. There have been several king-sized demonstrations against the test in Tokyo, the nearest major city to Amchitka. Politics, politics, politics.

The real question is: can we hack it for another whole month? After only eight days, we are smarting. We started out with enough fuel and supplies to last us six weeks, but Darnell says we've already gobbled up two weeks' worth of food. If the bomb does go off in early November – even the first of November – we will find ourselves at the tail end of the Aleutians, only a few hundred miles from the Soviet mainland, with a good two weeks between us and Vancouver. We'll have nothing to eat or drink and possibly not enough fuel to get there, what with the winter storms blowing down on us from the Bering Sea, and the Gulf of Alaska a convulsion of screeching winds. Bohlen figures we have three choices at this stage. One: we can turn around, go back to Vancouver, and wait until a new date for the test is announced. But they probably won't announce the date, or at least not until they have to, and Nixon only has to give something like seven days' warning. We can't possibly make it back up here in that time. Two: we can head in to Kodiak, park

Birmingham (left) and Cormack in the galley.

the boat, fly home, wait, then fly back up and carry on. But Cormack says you can't count on the weather at this time of year. It could take us as long as seventeen days to get from Kodiak to Amchitka, and if we pull into an American port, they may be able to pin us down in red tape. Three: we can keep going, try to find someplace in the Aleutians where we can get supplies, and kill time until we find out when the damn thing is going to go off.

We quibble and fret for hours. Somebody points out that at least the test has been delayed, which may be a victory of some kind. When was the last time a nuclear test was put off? Maybe we have the bastards on the run. If so, we have no choice but to keep up the pressure. And then up speaks one madman – me – who wants to press on straight to Amchitka, to go into orbit, as it were, around the island, and to go on a hunger strike until the test is cancelled. This idea doesn't exactly catch fire. "Are you kidding? Who'll run the boat?" Now our skipper comes down and announces that he thinks the hunger strike idea is great. "If you fellas aren't gobbling up all the food in sight, like you're doing now, there'll be more for me. And I can keep cooking up pancakes and chicken and fried eggs and bacon and porridge and ham and keep myself going for months. Then, as you fellas die off one by one, I'll throw your carcasses overboard and that'll cut down on the amount of bickering that's going on, *puh puh puh puh puh puh.*" He has the oddest laugh. We can never be certain that he isn't putting us on. In the end, after a long meeting while the boat flops this way and that, we decide to head for Kodiak.

FRIDAY, SEPTEMBER 24, 1971

Some of us climbed into our bunks last night thinking that in the morning we would wake up near the Alaska mainland. But the boat is back on course for the Aleutians. Bohlen and Metcalfe picked up some new information during the night and told Cormack to forget Kodiak. First, there is a military base there, and we might get trapped in red tape. Second, several reports have come in suggesting that the test will, *not* be delayed. Third, the Don't Make a Wave Committee is running low on funds and isn't sure it can afford to wait out the delay.

These are all good reasons to stay on course for Amchitka, but they don't get aired. A new kind of paranoia begins to develop, especially among the younger members of the crew. There are mutterings and grumblings about "unilateral decisions" having been made, but little of this comes out in the open. Officially Bohlen is our "leader." He is the only representative of the Don't Make a Wave Committee, the people who raised the money for the protest, got hold of the boat, chose the crew, and generally organized everything. As such, he has the right to make those kinds of decisions, although he keeps insisting that they are to be made by consensus. To adopt that method is to go walking barefoot on all the glowing coals of id and ideology. At the very least, we have set ourselves up for long hours of arguing and debating, finally to be driven back to lobbying and caucus meetings and strategy sessions and – yeah – it is a journey into politics, into all the boring familiar wrangling and power struggling. Bohlen has authority in this action, and he and Metcalfe – the two old vets from the Second World War – are on each other's wavelength, see themselves as the more mature men on board, and tend to make decisions on their own.

Another month on that boat! This trip is going to be at least a hundred times as heavy as I thought. I look down at Cummings, snoring in his bunk, and think, "Which one of us is going to crack first?" Some conflicts and lines of tension are already showing. Metcalfe can't stand Fineberg or Simmons, and neither of them can relate to Metcalfe. Cummings and I share an identity problem. For years I have wrestled with the question of whether to quit the Establishment press and go work for the underground press. People tell me, Don't be silly, you're much more effective working within the system, you reach more people with your ideas – legalization of dope, support for the Black Panthers and various Red Power groups, environmental revolution, and so on and so forth, up to and including the destruction of mental institutions and schools. The argument has substance. Why write to the converted? Still, it gnaws at me. Cummings, who works for the underground press, would be happier with my job – I think. The mirror image of yourself is the one you hate most, and we have already become the Alter Ego Kids. Cummings also seems to have caught some of the paranoia that infests the underground press, and that can be contagious.

Then there is the question of Fineberg and Simmons, both academics, versus Metcalfe, born during the Depression, when "If you didn't wake up with a hard-on on Christmas day, you didn't have anything to play with." He is the classic School of Hard Knocks grad, who scrambled his way up through the ranks in the bad old days of Canadian journalism, and he is a tough and competitive son of a bitch. One can imagine that way down in the bottomless existential depths of his mind there smoulders a special hatred of authority figures. My guess is that he was a demon at school, that above all he hated teachers, with their dreary logic and their tiresome power that derived solely from their mastery of blackboard psycho-gymnastics. Well, Fineberg and Simmons are teachers, all right. Both have come quickly, thoroughly to hate Metcalfe, and he in turn has got into the habit of shitting all over their logical rational analytical arguments the moment they open their mouths.

Scene: The Penthouse. Time: Four days out of Vancouver, coming up Grenville Channel, the afternoon that the Prime Minister is trying to reach us. I am at the wheel, quite stoned out by the miraculous natural beauty all around. Cummings wanders in from the upper deck and, like an actor stepping onstage, enters through the right doorway. (By

Fineberg.

this time we have already given up on "port" and "starboard." The first night out, Cummings asked the skipper which was which. "That's the left," Cormack snorted, "and that's the right. And that's straight ahead. Mostly we go straight ahead. Do you think you couple of thirty-three-pounders can remember that?") Cummings seems nervous. Or is he just acting nervous? I don't know – to me it seems that he is acting all the time. He is a columnist now, but he had worked as a detective for a while and now he is the president of the Georgia Straight Publishing Company because the editor is expecting an obscenity bust and thinks a good place for the president to be at a time like this is out at sea. He lights a cigarette and leans against the radar, staring straight ahead up the channel. Finally he says, "What's your opinion of Dick Fineberg?"

"He's beautiful," I reply, trying to avoid whatever's coming.

"No, seriously," says Cummings. "Hear me out." He wags his cigarette in the air to let me know he isn't kidding. "Nobody really knows him very well. We didn't check him out, you know. Have you noticed all the notes he's been taking?"

"You know what? I don't give a shit."

But Cummings is determined. "I'm beginning to think he's an agent for the CIA."

"That's ridiculous, man. Absolute crap. You have to be putting me on." He is talking about the guy who wrote *The Dragon Goes North*, which exposes U.S. Army germ warfare testing techniques in Alaska, the guy who was invited aboard the *Greenpeace* in the first place because of another exposé he wrote, about the thousands of tons of poison gas canisters that were dumped into the water not far from Amchitka – canisters that might be smashed by the blast, releasing all sorts of deadly shit into the air.

"No, I'm not. I've been watching him."

"Crap, man," I say. "Utter crap. Underground press paranoia."

Cummings gives up. "The trouble with you," he says, a parting shot, "is that you've never been busted. I have."

I go back to grooving in the slow passage of seamed rock faces and ballets of seeds sweeping down the channel. Moore had pointed to them earlier and said, "Just think, each one of those contains the complete genetic blueprint for a dandelion."

Thurston wanders in from stage left, camera slung over his shoulder like a tourist. He stands around for a while, fingers tugging at the point of his beard as always. Good old Doc. He's so cool and together – pure Consciousness III. I am just about to tell him the amusing story of Cummings' paranoia about Fineberg when he drops his voice, leans toward me, and says, "Listen, Booby, maybe I'm losing my mind, but there's a rumour going around that Fineberg is working for the CIA."

"Oh Christ, not you too, Doc!"

"Well, why not? Anything's possible, man. Put it this way: Do you believe a grand piano could come flying into the wheelhouse? Right now? Think about it."

"Well, sure. I mean, well, I guess an airplane or something *could* be passing over . . . the door *could* pop open . . . and a grand piano *could* . . . Sure. If you mean anything's possible, well, yeah, I'd have to be crazy to say it *couldn't* happen. Okay."

"Right on, Booby. There you are. I don't think Dick's a CIA agent, but what the hell? Grand pianos, man. That's where it's at. This boat's a grand piano when you think about it. A goddamn theatre critic and a saltchuck sea captain and a geodesic dome builder and, well, you can dig it. Why not a CIA agent thrown in just for the sheer cosmic beauty of it? The States is a crazy place, man. They do things like that, you know."

A few minutes after Thurston wanders off, enter Simmons from stage right. He's tied his glasses to his head with string to keep them from falling off in the high seas to come. "Have you been getting wind of the rumours about Fineberg?" he asks.

"Yep."

"Well, they're a bunch of crap, you know. Somebody's trying to discredit him. I have my suspicions about who it is, but I'm not saying – yet. The fact is, Fineberg's been raising some very good questions lately, and certain people don't want to deal with them."

"What good questions are those, Terry?"

"Well, for example, there is the very good question about our legal status when we get to Amchitka. Nobody knows. And nobody seems to want to know. Fineberg has been saying that we at least ought to get some lawyers working on it. He knows some good marine lawyers in Alaska who are willing to look into it for us. . . ." Simmons departs.

A while later, here comes Metcalfe, a copy of *The Strange Last Voyage of Donald Crowhurst* in his hand. "This is a hell of a book to be reading on a trip like this," he says. "You know, I don't know what it is, but I can't quite get it out of my head. There's something about Fineberg that bothers me. Have you noticed it? It's more of gut feeling than anything else. But . . . something."

Just as my turn at the wheel is ending, Bohlen saunters in, looking elfishly happy. "Great day, eh?"

"Sure. Listen, Jim. Have you been picking up on all these rumours about Fineberg?"

"What rumours?"

"About him being a CIA agent and all that shit."

"Uh-oh. Don't go spreading rumours like that." Christ, now I'm caught in it too. "Listen, man," says Bohlen, "I lived in the States too long not to be able to spot a CIA. Believe me, our boy Dick isn't the type."

"Well, you'd better do something to calm everybody down."

"Me? You do something. I want to look at the scenery. Come on, quit hogging the wheel. Isn't this something else?"

Climbing down the ladder to the bunkroom, I can hear Metcalfe,

Metcalfe at the radio. Bohlen looks on.

Simmons, and Fineberg arguing in the galley. To avoid the whole mess, I duck out the side door. Moore is out on deck, leaning against the forecastle wall, staring at the incredible mountains and forests flowing by. "Jesus," he says, "have you been picking up on all the bad vibes floating around about Dick Fineberg? Whew. He wouldn't be a CIA agent, would he? That would be *awful*."

Later, Fineberg comes out to the battenclaim and complains to Keziere and me that he's being shat all over every time he opens his mouth to make a logical point.

Still seasick, Keziere lifts his pale waste of a face and says, "Dick. This may not be the most logic-oriented crew you could ask for. But it just so happens that it's the only crew in a boat on its way to Amchitka right now, man. Either you can dig it or you can't."

"I see. Just keep my place, hmm?"

"No, that's not what I meant, man."

End of first paranoia scene.

Now we are nearing the Aleutians, faced with the likelihood that we will have to live one on top of another for at least another month, with the pressure getting heavier every day, Simmons and Fineberg permanently uptight about Metcalfe, Cummings and I glaring at each other like Dorian Grey and his portrait, and Metcalfe. . . . Well, the whole thing started when Fineberg posted a letter to his lawyer from Klemtu without showing it to any of us first. On Sunday Bohlen called a meeting and Metcalfe suggested that Fineberg might be an agent of the CIA or the Atomic Energy Commission. The meeting decided that he should stop working as a journalist aboard, and just serve as crew or cook. In Metcalfe's view, Fineberg created a bad feeling in the group by going his own way and lobbying Simmons and Keziere. Metcalfe and Bohlen made Fineberg send a telegram to his lawyer in Fairbanks, saying that the *Greenpeace* dissociated itself from Fineberg's letter and ordering him not to contact anyone aboard the *Greenpeace*, including

Fineberg. At that meeting, which got dubbed the Langara Episode for Langara Island, which we were passing at the time, Fineberg angrily denied being interested in the voyage as an exercise in journalism. But who among us could say what was really going on, deep in his own head? Could Metcalfe or Cummings or I deny all of our instincts as newsmen?

By that time, some fine levels of suppressed fury were at work. Simmons was outraged by Metcalfe – with justification, for he had been in on the planning of the voyage right from the beginning. He had had to hassle directly with the Sierra Club in the U.S. about it, because the Americans were slightly uptight about allowing the club's good name to be involved in such a reckless venture. During the two years from the time the scheme was hatched to the night the boat pulled away, Simmons had worked like a fanatic, on everything from high-level executive meetings to shifts on the forklift, loading fuel drums. He had put in hundreds of hours, often when other people were just wandering about dramatically, uttering profound thoughts. Metcalfe, on the other hand, had been involved in little of the manual toil that went into the preparation. So now it was all Simmons could do to stop himself from busting Metcalfe's teeth all over the deck.

Then there is the larger, more critical problem of the skipper and his feelings toward the whole lot of us – a trip in itself. Cormack is fifty-eight, the oldest guy on board. Next comes Birmingham, who is fifty-six. Then Metcalfe, fifty-two. Bohlen, forty-five. And then a decade drop to Thurston and Keziere, both thirty-four. Fineberg and Cummings, thirty-one. Me, twenty-nine (soon to traumatically turn thirty). Darnell and Simmons, twenty-five. Moore, twenty-four. Cormack went to sea in 1928 as a deckhand on the Union Steamship *Catala* and has been looking into the moods and rages of the ocean for longer than most of us have been alive. He is short, weighs 240 pounds, and is bald except for a wisp of white hair. His left hand is next to useless – "Only good for eating cookies." One finger ends just below where the fingernail should start. His right hand is a mess of seams and stitches. One day years ago, when he was out fishing, a nylon rope strong enough to bear twenty tons of tension had snapped, and the chain it was attached to exploded in Cormack's hands. He was thrown onto the deck, and even as he crashed down, he was thrusting both hands toward the sky. "Call a fuckin' airplane!" he roared, blood spurting from his smashed hands. Some crewmen threw up just at the sight of the bubbling squirting blood and bits of yellow bone sticking out of purple and black boils of skin. But Cormack was on his feet, bouncing from the deck like a rubber ball, hands flung heavenward, tromping into the galley, yelling at the cook to wrap his hands in towels. He sat there cursing steadily until a seaplane arrived, then clambered out into a skiff, hands still up in the air, and out to the plane. He rode all the way into the nearest port, then out of the plane and into a taxi, arms up like the branches of a tree with bloodstained nests at the top, and down to the hospital. Most men would have fled into unconsciousness or at least collapsed, but John Cormack – well, he has the survival reflexes of an old wild bull. If his head sometimes seems like a steel ball that has been ricocheting between iron walls for a century or two, it is only to be expected after the shit he must have gone through, hammering his way up from deckhand to shipowner in one of the most competitive hard-rock professions on earth. The few old skippers who have survived as long as Cormack are tough, that's all there is to it. Even at fifty-eight years of age he is strong enough to take on any of us and several combinations of us, and scatter us over the decks like children.

Cormack has a habit of being the last guy to come into the galley at suppertime. Three or four of us usually jam ourselves into the bench between the table and the back wall, and Cormack loves to carve out space for his huge bulk by freely chopping away at the nearest guy with his elbow, driving the lot of us down toward the other end of the

Hunter at the bow.

table. One morning, in a particularly bad mood, I made the mistake of thinking piss on this, you old bastard, I'm tired of being your punching bag, and when he started chopping at me with his elbow, I dipped into my own bag of tricks (a Purple Belt in Butokan Karate) and let him have a fairly solid side-handed chop in the ribs. There was a pause of about one-twentieth of a second while the skipper's eyes came level with mine – just enough time for me to realize that he had not made it to where he was by allowing himself to be beaten at anything, and *wham* – his elbow crunched back into my shoulder damn near hard enough to dislocate it. It would be a fight to the death or nothing. "Right, ah ha ha ha," I said. "You want me to move over? I'll move over."

Cormack is naturally suspicious of *pro*-fessors (Fineberg, Keziere, Simmons, Bohlen, Moore, and Darnell, who have degrees of one kind or another). He is also wary of *re*-porters (Metcalfe, Cummings, and me) – mainly because we were too eager, as we headed up the Inside Passage, to file stories about the engine suddenly conking out one morning. Any reference to his boat breaking down is like a slap on the face. He was so furious about one of Metcalfe's broadcasts that he threatened to throw us all off at Prince Rupert. But now we have been together long enough for him to sort us out according to our personalities, rather than our social roles, and he has become pretty comfortable with us. Except Thurston and Darnell. Darnell he can't stand. The rest of us think Darnell is doing a damn fine job of cooking, and he is a calm and stoic presence in the crew, but the skipper keeps muttering, "Now that Darnell fella – if this was a *regular* trip, I'd have fired him and kicked him off back at Alert Bay. Goddamn mattress lover, that's what he is. Calls that goop he serves us food. A cook like him wouldn't last two days on a *regular* fish run. . . ." As for Thurston, he's a doctor, and doctors are about as close to a priest class or a shaman or a wizard as you can get in Western society, so Cormack remains convinced that even if the rest of us are loonies, surely the doctor is a respectable gentleman. Yet here is this bearded shaggy-haired freak. Cormack keeps shaking his head. Can't figure it out, how a weirdo like that Lyle Thurston fella ever got to be a doctor.

Meanwhile, up in his bunk over the skipper, Fineberg is writing another letter to his lawyer in Fairbanks, complaining that we are shooting ourselves in the foot by not allowing the letter of the law to guide our strategy. Nobody is accusing him of being a CIA agent any more, but he is still an outsider. So is Cormack, which may be why the two of them hit it off so well, once Cormack stopped thinking of him as Dr Fineberg of the University of Alaska.

Or maybe it's simply because they are both candy freaks. Fineberg came aboard in Vancouver with boxes of chocolate and bags of candy, not knowing that the captain had a sweet tooth too – or, more precisely, four sweet teeth, the only teeth left in his mouth. We noticed early in the voyage that whenever anybody left a chocolate bar lying around, it disappeared. "Who's the chocolate bar thief?" we began to ask. It was one of the deeper mysteries of the voyage. "It's a CIA plot," said Fineberg, drily. Much later we learned that there was not just one chocolate bar thief on board, but two. I can just see them up in the radio room in the dark of night, whispering. "Pssssst, how many bars did ya cop today? I got three. Picked one from Hunter's pocket." "Good work. I got one from Moore while he was out taking a piss."

Poor Fineberg. As the only official American on board, he is a Big People (as in *Lord of the Rings*) and the rest of us, including the expatriate Bohlen, think of ourselves as Hobbits. It is totally unfair, ethnocentric, racist – the whole sorry bundle. Fineberg bears up quite gracefully, all things considered.

Thus divided, hung up, the seeds of mutiny already sown, late on a Friday afternoon, while far away some five thousand Canadians are blockading the U.S.–Canada border right across the continent from Vancouver to Fredericton in a protest against the test at Amchitka, we come within view of the Dread Mountains of Mordor.

The Aleutian Islands exist in a space warp or time warp or at least a culture warp, somewhere right outside the noosphere or the psychoelectronic skins of the Global Village. They come up out of the mists cold and bleak, like wrecks of giant grape-stained wine urns. Crags and slags and polished shards. Ocean heaving and running like foam through chipped and shattered tusk, froths on white-gummed beaches and a distant flush and whoosh of waves. With chunks of cliff coming into focus like a photo developing on hard-grain paper, it is as though we have stepped into a three-dimensional wraparound total immersion stereophonic movie about a little band of men armed only with magic electronic wands, going back and back in a funky seagoing time machine to the beginning of the planet, when volcanoes were still booming and chucking up bloodflows of planetary guts. That lurch in your vision may not be your optic nerve twitching, it may be the tic of yet another earthquake rumbling and clattering through the massive wreck-piles of stone and crumbled masonry, and the sea moaning as mountains shift their positions, jostling for a place to perch amid the cracks opening on the ocean floor.

It is a mist world of weird vibrations and dank cold creeping down from the fleets of icebergs in the Bering Sea. Last spring, blinding flashes of sunlight on ice were glancing into the eyes of the Aleut people whose villages are strung out through the islands. It was the first time in living memory that the icebergs had come so far south, like snow-queen chess pieces hundreds of feet high closing in on the ebony bishops and knights and castles of rock. A year ago, when I was in the Canadian Arctic as far north as Inuvik, the Inuit talked nervously about how, also for the first time in living memory, the whales failed to appear after spring breakup in the Mackenzie River delta. Here in the Aleutians, the Aleuts talk no less uneasily about the icefields travelling farther south than ever, jamming against the islands like ice

The *Greenpeace* enters the Bering Sea.

cubes pouring out of a freezer that cannot stop pumping them out. The mood is intensifed by the islands' "high ambient strain fields" – they are the most geologically unstable area on earth, the epicentre of the great Alaska earthquake of 1964. And now Cannikin is soon to roar among the volcanoes, its vibrations crashing through the earthquakes that occur almost daily in the region. It is as though the plot of the wraparound movie hangs on the theme of a world coming to its end. Whales failing to appear, icebergs on the march, suspected submarine rumbling – an impression of the temples of Atlantis collapsing in bursts of bubble and trailing slime, far beneath us in the icy grey water. The pale purple ghost of a giant jellyfish floats past the bow like a cellophane bag, a nexus of nerve-webs in the centre. At any moment a dull red flare could pulse through the fog as one of the volcanoes booms to life.

We go through Unimak Pass in the dark, and Cormack insists on taking the wheel himself until we are almost into the Bering Sea. Between the broken flanks of mountain on either side of the pass, uncountable tons of water rush from the sea into a mad embrace with the surges coming up from the Gulf of Alaska, generating rip tides that can tear the steel boat apart like a toy. Up until this point, Cormack has got his jollies telling us sea stories that made our hair stand on end, and when twenty- and thirty-foot swells roared across the Gulf at us like steamrollers, he laughed and said, "Huh, that's fuck all. It's when the waves get as high as treetops, that's when a fella gets to thinking." With the twenty- and thirty-foot swells, the rest of us have got to thinking quite a bit. What thoughts will we have later on? Now, as we crawl gingerly through Unimak Pass, Cormack is no longer laughing. "Some fellas was up here last winter," he says, "and they damn near got caught in the biggest damn rip tide you ever saw. Water just suddenly split. Dropped seven feet on one side and stayed up on the other. Damn near got caught. A couple of steel boats I know of got ripped right in half getting caught in one of those."

So he isn't about to leave amateurs at the helm. He stays up all night, handling the wheel as though it were an eggshell, leaning forward the whole time with his head cocked slightly sideways, pressing all his senses down into the hull, feeling, groping, jiggling, flicking the wheel like a man guiding an elephant along a high wire. The swells have subsided, but there is almost a hum in the night air, a strange gurgling sound rising up all around the boat. "A lot of good men have gone down in this here pass," Cormack says. But mainly he doesn't talk much, just hangs in there at the wheel, sensitive as a bat creeping through a monster-haunted cave. Well, we have made it to the Bering Sea. But there is a new problem. (There is always a new problem.) Seems Cormack needs to do some work on the engine – tightening something here, replacing a few pins, pumping out the bilge – the sort of work he can't do when the boat is tumbling around in the open sea, and seeing as how we can expect the weather to get worse and worse, he figures we'd better do it while we can. That screws up all our hopes of staying out of jurisdictional reach of the Americans – there are no non-American ports around that we can put into – but it has to be done.

Metcalfe gets on the radio and establishes contact with the U.S. Coast Guard ship *Balsam*, which is somewhere in the vicinity, and requests permission to put in at Dutch Harbor, just around the corner of Unimak Pass on Unalaska Island. A reply comes back to the effect that Dutch Harbor is a U.S. Navy base, so the request will have to be forwarded to the Navy, and the Navy will want to know all our names, nationalities, etc. In the meantime we are to anchor and wait for clearance. We come out of Unimak Pass into the Bering Sea at about four in the morning, swing north around Akun and Akutan islands, and drop anchor three miles off Akutan, just across Akutan Pass from Unalaska Island. Then we wait twenty-four hours for word to come from the U.S. Navy via the Coast Guard cutter *Balsam*, which we have already renamed the *Pisscutter Ballsoff*.

Sunday, September 26, 1971

Last night Metcalfe broke out a bottle of rum he had stashed away, and we had a party. We had reached the Bering Sea and we were within 400 miles of Amchitka. Emperor Hirohito had arrived in Anchorage and Nixon had gone to greet him, and while we drank and sang in the galley, squawks of sound came bursting through the old wooden radio box mounted on the galley ceiling – crowds cheering and chanting, excited announcers babbling about this "historic moment," the Emperor of Japan landing on North American soil for the first time in the history of the known universe. Not a word about the Second World War, when 30,000 Japanese stormed the Aleutian Island of Attu, just two days' sailing beyond Amchitka – apparently one of the greatest battles of the war, yet it was fought in a blackout. Neither the United States nor Canada could admit to their people that the dread yellow hordes had established a beachhead on the edge of continental North America. The Japanese refused to surrender or give up an inch of territory, and the battle raged for ten days. In the end, the Japanese were wiped out to a man, all 30,000 of them.

But now the Emperor of the Rising Sun was shaking Richard Nixon's hand in Anchorage and the mindless mobs were cheering. We had vaguely hoped that the Emperor would say something like: "Say, Dick, it's kind of a rotten thing you're doing up at Amchitka, blowing off a bomb 250 times the size of the one you dropped on us at Hiroshima, and just a couple of thousand miles away from the wobbly earthquake-prone heart of Tokyo, which you may remember is the largest city in the world. . . ." But the Emperor said nothing. Nixon said nothing. The gushing announcers said nothing. There were no demonstrations, no outcries. Just Nixon's voice squawking through the old wooden radio in the galley, talking about the eternal friendship that has endured "between our two great peoples. . . ." And then, in a small lame voice,

On the open sea.

"for the last quarter of a century." Politics, politics, politics.

Darnell reached out and savagely clicked off the radio. We downed the rum, and – ho ho! – a couple more bottles of wine were found. Moore opened a can of lemon juice upside down and Cummings screamed, "After ten days at sea haven't you fucking learned not to open cans upside down?" We sang a couple of rounds of "Bering Sea" to the tune of "Deep Blue Sea," then a few verses of "I Left My Heart at Old Amchitka," and generally got ourselves plastered. Fineberg broke out his banjo, Darnell went to work on his harmonica, Thurston and I hammered away on some pots and pans, the galley was thick with fumes from our smokes. "We love you, Greenpeace, Oh yes we do, *Oooohhhh Greenpeace, we love you. . . .*"

This morning, suffering badly from the runs and a hangover, I stagger from my bunk and find Metcalfe unconscious in the galley, slumped in a canvas camping chair, still in his red ᴛ-shirt, his woollen ski cap perched at a jaunty angle on his head. The boat is rolling at maybe a fifteen-degree angle, the rum bottle clanks down from one end of the galley floor to the other like a glass rat, everything is in motion – yet somehow Metcalfe remains perfectly balanced, his head on one shoulder, his goatee resting like a blue jay on his collarbone, his centre of gravity just low enough that he remains stable while the galley, the boat, the whole world goes lurching and swinging around him. The party was good for us. Nobody has quite realized how much tension we were storing up as we came across the Gulf, and now we have blown it all out.

The galley is a mess. Cigarette butts, punched-open cans, dented pots and pans, crumbs, the remains of a jigsaw puzzle that someone from the United Church of Canada gave us scattered all over the floor. Early in the planning stages of the protest, the church considered sending a ship it happened to own – a ship much larger than the *Phyllis Cormack* – to Amchitka with us. But they backed off on the advice of the ship's captain. The waters around Amchitka are considered to be among the most dangerous in the world because of the rip tides, and the Aleutians are the nesting place, as it were, of a strange meteorological phenomenon known as a williwaw, a hurricane-force wind that blows up out of nowhere, then vanishes. Such winds have been known to tear the wheelhouses off boats ten times the size of ours. They stalk the Aleutians like weird demons of wind. Because of these factors, combined with the possibility of a radiation leak or a shock wave from the blasts, the church concluded that it could not take such risks with human lives, even for such a good cause. Well, that was cool. But too bad the United Church doesn't have the vigour of, say, the Quakers, who in 1958 twice sent boats out – the *Phoenix* and the *Golden Rule* – against atmospheric nuclear tests, in the face of certain death. Neither Quaker boat reached its destination – one got pinned down in red tape at the dock and the other got grabbed at sea by the U.S. Navy. We are on a Canadian boat and most of us are Canadians, so the Americans can't grab us on the open seas as they could grab the American Quakers. We had ignored the puzzle until last night, then we drunkenly put it together, only to discover that it said GOD BLESS YOU. Down to the floor it was flung with a vengeance. "Why doesn't somebody send a telegram to the United Church, thanking them for sending a jigsaw puzzle instead of a boat?"

But in the morning, the bad feeling toward the United Church dissolves. It is Sunday, and Dorothy Metcalfe gets through on the radio to let us know that the head office of the United Church in Toronto has authorized the ringing of church bells across the country in a protest against the Amchitka test. More to the point, they will be saying prayers for our souls. And then we get word from the *Pisscutter Ballsoff* that the U.S. Navy has turned down our request to put in at Dutch Harbor, but we may go into Akutan.

"Huh," says Cormack. "I was in Dutch Harbor when they set that last bomb off at Am-cheet-ka back in '69, and nobody said anything then about it being a military base." But back then he was an ordinary Canadian fisherman. Now he is the skipper of CAN VES GREEN PEACE, a whole different scene. Up comes the anchor and back we chug around Akutan Island. The Authorized Prayer from Toronto must be working – the sun slashes open the cloud banks and scatters them in drifts and plumes across the sky. The vegetation that hugs the island above the cliffs is like a fur hide, a shade of green that none of us has ever seen. "We'll call that Greenpeace green," says Bohlen. We are all out on deck, hauling in lungfuls of vintage wine-sparkling air, and the surface of the ocean is thick with herring gulls, petrels, black-legged kittiwakes, horned puffins, sooty shearwaters, slender-billed shearwaters, and ducks and terns of all kinds. Whitecaps lick among them, and as the boat dives forward they rise in sweeps, like parts of a single immense body flapping and cruising over the water. I have never seen so many birds in my life. Their cries are all around, splintering on the gusts of wind as crab pots dance on the waves, sea lions bob up in packs of half a dozen and roll and flop alongside us, seals, porpoises, jellyfish, hundreds of thousands of birds flapping in cloud banks, the waters breaking around brown- and black-furred animal persons that leap and plunge everywhere.

Moore runs from one end of the boat to the other with *Peterson's Field Guide to Western Birds* in one hand and binoculars in the other, yelling, "Wow – that one over there! With the big bright orange beak and the white cheek markings on a black body, that one! That's a . . . that's a . . ." *flip flip flip* through the pages, ". . . a *crested puffin!* Isn't it beautiful? Jesus Christ, what a heaven! Oh, I want to live here the rest of my life!" At certain moments the sky and the green carpets of the islands appear only as flashes of colour between surging waves of feather, and the sound of all those birds envelops the boat so completely that we have to shout to make ourselves heard. Into Akutan Bay we chug, and far down the neck of the bay is a tiny cluster of little white wooden houses, all with green roofs, like a mushroom patch. Already we are becoming aware of something peculiar to the Aleutians – the grass grows as high as your knees, as high as your thighs in a few places, but there are no trees at all – only moss and fungus clinging to the rocks, and spruce that grows like bonsai, never getting any taller than three or four inches. Streams come sparking down between trenches and gorges carved in the bedrock, but beyond the castle-like cliffs there is nothing that you can take a bearing on to gauge distances. If there were any trees here, or buildings on the slope, we could guess how far away a given hill or pasture or meadow is. But all the usual visual reference points are unavailable, so a hill that seems only a few thousand yards away may actually be five miles off across the slopes, and a meadow that appears to be an hour's walk away may be reachable in ten minutes.

The surf-cloud at Akutan Bay, Alaska.

Akutan

The experience of arriving in Akutan Bay is a bit like landing on Mars – it is another world and the mind wobbles in confusion, suddenly not knowing how big the world is or how small. No sooner does Cormack let down the anchor about a hundred yards away from the village than we shove the skiff overboard and scramble to be the first to go ashore. The mountains and meadows beckon. We have been eleven days at sea now, and we have developed a thirst, a raging hunger to get back on the land. *And look where we are!* Beyond the village, a smooth, lush Greenpeace green hide of moss and grass rambles up toward a dark flat-topped mountain (1,650 feet high, according to the maps) with a plate-glass sky beyond so bright it shrinks our pupils to pinpoints. On the other side of the bay – well, mountains, but they are completely blanketed in clouds unlike any clouds we have ever seen. The Surf-Cloud of Akutan, streaming over the mountains like an endlessly breaking wave, a wide foamy froth of white smoke, flowing boiling sluicing plummeting in absolute silence down the slopes until it reaches the water and then somehow vanishes as though into a hidden crack in the earth. Such a torrent of cloud must soon exhaust itself – but no, the Surf-Cloud keeps coming, rushing magically down the slopes, rimming the mountains with white gauze, a silent unending downward surge like the granddaddy of perpetual tidal waves looming over the bay. It is . . . *awesome*.

And now that we are out in the air and streaking for the land, wide sky scaled down by the green mountain on one side and the Surf-Cloud on the other, the crankiness and claustrophobia are released and we are wild and free as children escaping from a dungeon. Like Alice, we have passed through the looking glass. After a week on the cold grey-silver-white shadows of the Gulf, in a single step we have entered a realm as unbearably intense and brilliant as the Other Worlds of schizophrenia and LSD, flashing explosions popping from rapier blades of grass, stalks thrusting bunchberries at us like tiny brain creatures, rainbows unfurling beyond the Surf-Cloud, alien civilizations of cow parsnips arrayed at our feet, moss, lupine, horsetails, blueberries, and daisies like scattered flaming bits of Holy Nimbus. It is a psychedelic rush – one moment staggering through the stupor of battered turned-off senses, then *click* – the music is on, you are on, the universe leaps eagerly and joyously to embrace you, to let loose the fireworks in the middle of your brain, tell you all its secrets at once, infuse every flower petal and every bead of water with neon – look, look, look. And down goes your mind like a tree in an avalanche, crashing into a state of grace, a beyond-words orgy of seeing and feeling and smelling and hearing – ah, and above all, of being. All there, not somewhere else, not locked away in a time capsule in your head, but turned inside out, in touch at last, touching, being touched by, in touch with what is around you. We're out of that dinky little boat, where the reek of our unwashed bodies has become a palpable gas in which we float, hardly able to breathe, nothing but grey and silver and black outside the portholes, and shadows, dark wood, peeling varnish, rust, green metal, and grease-soaked floors within. From that we come to this, from a universe with three dimensions to one with at least fifty. Pow! Thurston throws out his arms and screams, "Far *out!*" as he jumps from the skiff onto the gravel shore. He is looking up at the great green rippling mountain universe before us, above us, around us and all over, like the beard of a green giant. "*Unreal*," Moore whispers, clambering out beside him. "Too much," says Cummings. "*Out* of sight, man," says Keziere, and on the shores of Akutan we speak the language beyond the Age of Literacy, as precise a language as we can find.

We walk into the Aleut village feeling like we are in a Bergman film. The path leading up from the beach has taken us past a dock where a cannery boat is moored and straight through the local graveyard, wet ornate stones and mouldering wooden crosses overseen by a Russian Orthodox church, left over from the days before the Americans bought up Alaska, when the fleets of the Czars swept down among the islands. Of the 10,000 Aleuts who lived here when the Russian warships arrived, all but 120 were killed. About 3,500 people remain, scattered in seventeen communities throughout the 1,100 islands. Their history goes back 8,000 years. Here as elsewhere, in the wake of the sword and the cannon, came the cross – in this case, the double-barred cross of the Russian Orthodox Church. Would the Americans be participating in this protest if the Soviets had held on to the islands and were themselves planning to set off an underground nuclear explosion? This is a strange land of cultural overlap, a devastated group of Native people, once massacred by Russians, who are now the arch-foes of the Americans, who are about to blast off a bomb right under the asses of the Aleuts.

The clearest thought that comes out of all this is: Jesus, I wouldn't want to be an Alley-oot. The village looked enchanted when we were pulling in aboard the *Greenpeace* – small white shoebox houses with their green roofs – but as we got closer we could see that it was much like the Native communities along the west coast of B.C. Broken-down shacks were scattered along the shoreline and wrecked boats lay on the beaches. The only paid work left for the Aleuts is to chop up Alaska

Hunter.

king crab on the cannery boat, and a bit of fishing. But the fish are dying off and the whaling station across the bay has long since been closed down. One by one the Aleuts are being forced onto welfare. The same dreary story of a rich land looted by the white man and his technology, then abandoned when the game is up. We pass through the village quickly, bearing the white man's burden of guilt. An old Aleut man sits on a swing overlooking the bay. One of his hands ends in a mechanical contraption, a variation on the old hook, complex enough for him to hold a cigarette between two of the metal parts.

"Hi," I say. "Beautiful weather you've got here."

"Been bad, been bad. Bad weather. First time the sun's shone since spring. Not a day of sun all summer. Very bad."

"You mean today's the first time you've seen the sun since *spring?*"

"Bad. Bad weather. Yep."

"Well, I guess you don't know about it, but that boat we're on, with the green sail, that's the *Greenpeace*. We're up here to, ah, protest against the, ah, bomb that's gonna be set off up at Amchitka – you know about that?"

"Yep. We know. Weather's been bad ever since they set off the last one."

"Right on. Well, anyway, the United Church of Canada said some prayers for us today. So I guess all this beautiful weather is a miracle, eh?"

No reply. He just looks away, shakes his head, lifts the cigarette to his mouth and then blows out some smoke without having inhaled. "Bad. Bad."

Later we learn that he's the local lay preacher for the Russian Orthodox Church, and we hear that with some indignation he has complained to people in the village that one of those funny-looking men from the protest boat has been going around claiming that

The *Greenpeace* off Akutan Island, Alaska.

the weather's a miracle brought on by prayers from another church thousands of miles away. That doesn't make us any more popular in the village. But whatever popularity we may have earned is about to be destroyed forever. Just after we pass through the village, Moore, Bohlen, Keziere, Simmons, Darnell, Fineberg, and I take off madly up the hill, whooping and bounding. The slopes are snaggled with tundra and scrub willows and moss – a mattress of vegetation, a tough springy miniature forest over which we leap like giants. We lurch drunkenly, discovering that we haven't got our land legs yet. This vegetation is like a trampoline – you can take seventeen-foot leaps and bounce. You can throw yourself around crazily and not get hurt. With the wind slapping our cheeks, and explosions of plant smells engulfing the salt and stink of our clothes and bodies, we flounder up the hill and follow a stream until we are up maybe 600 feet over the village and presumably out of sight. Then, in a flash, we are tearing off our clothes and crashing into the – *Ah! My God, it's cold!* – stream. The finest goddamn experience in my life, lying there in a gravel creek bed in about five inches of sloshing icy water, under a blinding ultra-blue sky. The wind flattens the grass, the Surf-Cloud rolls along, the crust of sweat and salt on my body is washed away, and my itchy sticky hair floats as free as seaweed around my head. There are three sinks on the boat, but there is so little water that we are under strict orders not to use water for anything but cooking and drinking, except half a cup daily to brush our teeth. One by one the other guys peel off their clothes and get in the water – Darnell crashing in with a whoop, Moore easing in, Bohlen lowering himself with a gritty-toothed grin, Fineberg cautiously moving upstream to ensure that he is completely out of sight of the village.

Back in my clothes, I kneel on the slope by the stream, arms thrown toward the sky, and offer a prayer to Mother Earth, who is now Lover Earth. "You're so beautiful, lady. I love you! Love the Earth! Ohhhhhhhh, man, this is without doubt the most beautiful planet in the universe. It has to be. *God, I love her. . . .*" It is a feeling that only a zombie could go through life without experiencing, a feeling that comes in a flash on a wild wet afternoon, or during a storm or a blizzard, or in the spring or fall or on a sleepy heat-wrapped summer afternoon – a feeling of *planet love*. Different from love for children, different from love for a woman or a man, different from love for a special pet, and way beyond love of country. Planet love. It is such a miracle of planetary art, this gleaming gem of Earth. Or maybe all of those feelings of love radiate from a single inner source. Maybe the problem is that we categorize, chop up the surges of life-awareness into little hunks, because who can feel the whole thing without blowing up? Under my wet knees the grass and the moss and the scrub willows sink toward a mushy embrace with the rocks of the island, to the seabeds, which spread around the globe like palpitating tissue, and there is no point on Earth where anything is divided or sundered from anything else. "I *am* the Earth!" Moore standing there dripping wet, grinning at my delicious madness, his eyes roving lovingly over the plants.

When we get back to the boat, Metcalfe tells us that the stream we bathed in is the water supply for the village, and that at least one woman there has announced that she won't take another drink of water until those filthy men from the protest boat go away. We have to stay in Akutan for six days, waiting for word on the new date for the detonation of the bomb. There is only one telephone on the island, a radiophone down at the grocery store. The ship radio can't get anything out through the mountains around us, and the radiophone hookup is part of an inter-island party line. The main generator is over on Unalaska Island at Dutch Harbor, and each island is allowed a ration of telephone time per day. With Metcalfe, Cummings, Fineberg, and I all wanting to file dispatches, press releases, reports, and columns, and at least 120 Aleuts in the village who may also want to use the phone, we have a big logistics problem. Metcalfe has priority – he is in charge of relaying press releases. The rest of us will have to wait until Friday morning, when the mail plane arrives for its once-a-week pickup. Meanwhile, Simmons and Bohlen do what they can in their few moments on the radiophone, calling the Don't Make a Wave Committee in Vancouver and representatives of various environmental groups in Washington, D.C. *When is the bloody bomb going to go off?*

Cormack figures we are only four or five days from Amchitka if we have decent weather, but we can't just go straight to the island and wait. This is something we didn't understand before – the storms of the autumn equinox will soon be upon us, and there is no way the boat can survive out in the open water. "The way fishermen work it up here," says Cormack, "is you wait for a break in the weather, then you rush out as far as you can, put down your pots or your nets, then high-tail it back to shelter before one of them williwaws or a storm comes up. Wait again for another break in the weather, then make a run for it, grab up your gear, and get going back to port fast as you can. Weather's mean up here this time of year. So far we've been lucky. That weather you fellas thought was so bad out on the Gulf, shit, that was nothing. That was the flattest calm I've seen in forty years out there this time of year. But she'll start getting sloppy now. Getting close to October."

"So we can't just get going now and wait it out?"

"For a whole month? Shit, no. Never last. Not unless we can run for shelter when the wind comes up."

"We can't do that. It's a security zone around Amchitka. They won't let us in, that's for sure."

"Well then, you fellas are just gonna have to sit on your hands and sweat it out. Nothing else you can do. Now we'll see how much of what you'd call *staying power* ya got . . . *puh puh puh puh puh.*"

Frantically, Bohlen, Simmons, and Metcalfe put through their calls, scratching like dogs for a single scrap of information: *when?* The reports are contradictory. Some sources say late October. Others insist it will be November at the earliest. Environmentalists in Washington are "confident" that they have the Atomic Energy Commission on the run. They are attacking on every possible legal front. According to the White House, Nixon is "studying" the test. Six "leading scientists," including former presidential aides, have come out against it because of "physical and political risks." Cannikin, they say, is "potentially the most destructive man-made underground explosion in history." Former U.S. Secretary of State Dean Rusk says he believes a majority of Americans are against it. The U.S.–Canada border has been blockaded. Relations with Japan may be damaged, according to Alaska Senator Mike Gravel. One day the newspapers carry reports that Nixon is "seriously considering" cancelling the test. The next day the headlines read: N-BLAST STILL ON. *The Saturday Review* and *The New York Times* have spoken out against it. In Ottawa there is talk of sending an all-party Canadian delegation to Washington to make a plea to Nixon. External Affairs Minister Mitchell Sharp lodges what he calls a "forceful presentation" of Canada's views on Cannikin with U.S. Secretary of State William Rogers. Then, under pressure from American environmental groups, the United States Court of Appeals orders a lower court to reconsider an earlier ruling allowing the test. While the ruling does nothing to stop the blast, it does force the issue back into the courts. Like a seesaw, the battle swings back and forth. Meanwhile we continue to scrap and claw desperately for one tiny nugget of pure information: *when?*

By this time the boat has become home. Damn uncomfortable overcrowded home, but home, and we are starting to love it for its sheer funkiness. Certain things have become fixtures in our lives: the photo poster of an atomic mushroom cloud pinned up in the doorway from the galley, opposite a Sierra Club poster with the motto: IN WILDNESS IS THE PRESERVATION OF THE WORLD. And another poster, intended for display should we get busted by the Coast Guard, which says simply, in big black letters: MANGE D'LA MARDE. (We looked around for a

FUDDLE DUDDLE poster, in reference to the famous expletive mouthed by Trudeau in the House of Commons, but they were all sold out.) In the bunkroom, junk has begun to accumulate in the corner between the bunks. Seashells, rocks, bits of driftwood, bones, barnacles, crab shells – we are hopeless souvenir addicts. Metcalfe, Moore, and I have slung curtains across our bunks to give us a measure of privacy, and Cormack took one look and pronounced them jerk-off curtains. In the galley dangle plastic peace pennants thrown to us by the kids at Klemtu, and the blurred face of Richard Nixon continues to look out over all our meetings and meals and conversations and arguments.

Then somebody in the village learns that we have a doctor on board, and a couple of the men come out to the boat to ask Thurston to examine a friend of theirs who has some horrible sickness. Back and forth the friend has been shuttled between Akutan and hospitals in Anchorage and Juneau, and each time he's been sent back with the stark diagnosis of chronic alcoholism. But Thurston doesn't know this at the time and he doesn't mind improving our relations with the villagers, especially since we may be here for another month. It is rainy on the night he goes into the village with the two Aleuts. The sick guy is drunk by the time they arrive at his house. He complains of chest pains, back pains, stomach pains, head pains, the works. Catching on fast, Thurston figures he can get himself out of the whole mess by insisting on a urine test. It is a neat ploy. To conduct a urine test he needs a microscope, and he hasn't brought one along and doubts that anyone on the island has one. Out into the rain staggers the patient to piss in a beer bottle, at which point his two friends suddenly remember that the schoolteacher – the only white resident on the island – has a microscope. By this time they've plied Thurston with a few shots of rye and he's a bit wobbly himself. They all goes off into the rain, the patient merrily waving around his bottle full of piss, his two pals laughing and stumbling all over the place, Thurston saying to himself, "What am I doing?"

Metcalfe.

They arrive well past midnight. The teacher is an uptight, totally straight old cat who brags that he hasn't read a newspaper in thirty years and whose classroom walls are plastered with posters bearing messages like THIS IS YOUR FLAG – BE PROUD OF IT. Earlier this week he told Keziere and Metcalfe that the whole bunch of us ought to pack it up and go home since the bomb is none of our business (hello out there, John Wayne!), and that if it weren't for America, the Commies would long since have taken over the world and made everybody into slaves like the Cubans. Now his doorbell rings in the night and three stoned Aleuts stand on his doorstep, one of them holding a beer bottle that he claims is full of urine. Thurston, who looks quite deranged, explains that he's a doctor and he wants to borrow the school's microscope to run a urine test to find out what's wrong with this fellow here, whom the teacher knows is the village lush. Teach gumbles and swears but this crazy-looking foreigner is an actual doctor, so he takes them to the school. Thurston runs the urine test, mumbles some Latin incantations and says he'll have to look some things up in one of his medical books back on the boat. Then everybody crashes and fumbles back out into the rain, and the teacher swears at them as they fade away into the night. "From now on," says Thurston, "if anybody wants to know what I do for a living, tell them I'm a fucking botanist. Got it?"

We have also discovered that the young guys in the village hate whites with a passion. It makes no difference to them whether we're Canadians or Americans, for the bomb or against it – we're white. As they walk past us on the wooden planks running through the village (the only road), they make a point of spitting on the boards. Several beautiful young women live here too, and they seem extremely friendly. When Cummings mentions this – "Strictly as an observation, you understand" – the skipper points out that there is a $1,000 fine if you get caught with an Aleut women on board your boat, even if she's not doing anything at all. The Aleuts are penned in here like animals. They are forced to slave away for rotten wages on the crab cannery boat, and when the boat pulls out at the end of the season there is nothing for the adults to do but sit around and drink, which they do with a vengeance. After a few days we start to avoid the village, because every time we go there, somebody invites us in for a drink, and once you've accepted one drink you are expected to accept a second and a third and a fourth. After a couple of occasions of crawling back to the shore in the wee hours of the morning, head swirling and vomit boiling up in your throat, calling out hoarsely to the *Phyllis Cormack*, "Hey! Will somebody please come out and get us? *Heeeeeyyyy!* Anybody awake? Ahoy, the Greenpeace! Hey, wake up you bastards! Come and get me before I freeze to death! *Send that skiff out, f'Christ's sakes!*", you get into the habit of staying away from the village.

But not from the mountains and the meadows beyond. We are, after all, nature freaks. Simmons founded the Sierra Club of B.C. – considered in the U.S. to be the northern lunatic fringe, but still a part of the Club. Bohlen and Darnell are directors. They subscribe to the motto IN WILDNESS IS THE PRESERVATION OF THE WORLD, and Bohlen keeps saying that this territory, the Aleutians, is authentic Sierra Club land. It is wild and nearly unspoiled, a perfect place to get back in touch with the Earth.

MONDAY, SEPTEMBER 27, 1971

Simmons, Bohlen, and Darnell announce that they are going to lead a Sierra Club expedition up to the top of the 1,650-foot hill rising beyond the village. Does anybody else want to come along? Moore, Fineberg, Cummings, Keziere, and I decide to join them. At 8 a.m., after a whopping breakfast, Birmingham shuttles us ashore in relays, equipped with all the sandwiches and smokes we can carry, and we set out. By this time the slope is wrapped in fog, the bad weather having returned after being driven away briefly by the Authorized Prayer from Toronto. We are all wearing green jackets with hoods that were supplied by the Don't Make a Wave Committee, so it looks as though we are in uniform. And we are. Think of the army for which we are the troops. The Vancouver Real Estate Board paid for TV commercials showing a sudden earthquake and nuclear explosion, urging its viewers to STOP THE TEST AT AMCHITKA – a giant step, and with such heavy artillery. The Americans are catching up! No one can doubt the power of advertising. If presidents and cigarettes and booze can be marketed successfully on TV, why not peace? This may be the first time such an attack has been launched on the military Establishment. "*What?* A bunch of guys right out of the Chamber of Commerce attacking us with the same heavy commercials they use to peddle pantyhose?" Military intelligence must be cringing at that one, the Establishment turning their own big guns on themselves. Metcalfe has been in public relations long enough to understand the tricks of Mad Avenue. In modern Western industrial society, power rolls not out of the barrel of a gun but out of the cathode ray tube. And so he did not hesitate to welcome aboard as temporary allies even the "land sharks." I almost decided not to go when I first saw that commercial ("Christ, if *those* guys are on our side!"). But advertising is power – only a fool would refuse to unleash it on his enemies – and the U.S. military-industrial complex is our enemy and our children's enemy. Revolution makes strange bedfellows, such as the Sierra Club and the Vancouver Real Estate Board, but then again, if the world gets wiped out, you won't get a plug nickel for a chunk of terrestrial real estate.

So, as we climb Akutan Mountain in our green uniforms, we laugh. We are soldiers in the Army of the Landlord as well as the shock troops of the Conservation Movement. Up and up and up we climb, and a white kitten from the village follows along behind us. The rain sheets

The *Greenpeace* anchored in Akutan Bay, Alaska.

down the slopes, the grass is slippery and wet and cold to the touch, and the wind is chill enough to remind us of those ice packs not far away in the Bering Sea. Yet the kitten tags along and keeps up. Where I come from, that's not how kittens behave. "Another grand piano, man," says Thurston. Cummings picks up the kitten lovingly, and for the first time in a week I start to like him. Oh, the vibes are starting to get good.

Bohlen and Darnell are so far ahead they're almost lost in the fog rolling down on us. All the synchs and weird combinations that have been gathering since we set out start to click in our heads. We are the green-hooded men: Captain Cormack's Lonely Hearts Club Band, the Fellowship of the Piston Rings, Soldiers of the Landlord, the Unofficial Official Canadian Navy, Eight Angry Environmentalists, the Warriors of the Rainbow, the Crew of the *Friendship Frigate*, the Crew of the *Greenpeace*, the Akutan Branch of the Moody Blues Fan Club, the Bearers of the One Ring of Ecology, the Unconventional Symbol of All Canada's Revulsion at the Amchitka Test. The United Church has prayed for our souls and the Prime Minister has blessed us. We are the underground press and the Establishment press, the crew of the National Film Board, a flying wedge of freaks and straights – multisensory mutants and middle-class protestors, all slogging together through bursts of icy rain, fog all around us, the world itself vanished, leaving us wandering across a broken-off chunk of Earth sailing through a grey mist of cosmic voids, all singing, "We love you, Greenpeace, Oh yes we do . . . oooooohhhh, Greenpeace, we love you."

Somebody gets an inspiration and yells, "All power to the plants!"

"Right on!"

"Who are we?"

"We're the Green Panthers!"

Then a greater inspiration: "Hawkaaaaa! *We're the Greenhawks!*" That's it. The Greenhawks, leaping through a non-world of fog, clambering up on outcroppings of rock and throwing ourselves off in mad leaps, landing on a great natural trampoline of scrub willow and mush and blueberries and springing up into the air again, curling, rolling over and over down the slope, wrestling with each other like kids, screaming *"Hawka!"* just like the Blackhawks in the old comics used to do when they went on the attack. "Everything's getting unreal again," Moore sings out. For we have got such a contact high that our minds have begun to mesh. We make flashing instantaneous connections with each other, as though a Group Mind had begun to form – the sort of thing Tielhard de Chardin and Marshall McLuhan talk about. Where does one Greenhawk stop and the other begin? Is a new race in the making? Not just here, with the eight Merry Men in their green Sherwood Forest uniforms, but *out there* in the world beyond the enveloping fog, a race whose midwife is the transpolitical alliance being forged to stave off the impending destruction of the world? Metcalfe isn't with us on this mystical journey, but I can almost hear him yelling from the boat, *"Beware of paranoid grandiosity!"*

But . . . but . . . but . . . couldn't the Greenhawks be the forerunner of an army in the making? The Army of the Earth? Just this month the United Nations declared the beginning of World War Three, a war against industrial and military pollution of the planet. "Ben!" I am yelling to Metcalfe in my mind, through the fog. "It might be real!" And if it's not, if there's no new mass alliance of forces rising up to reverse the self-destructing forward rush of the Megamachine, then there's no hope. And man, I've still got hope! I can't live without it. We are the famous poster, GET HIGH ON A MOUNTAIN.

How high nobody can tell because of the swirling grey-as-the-inside-of-your-brain fog, but we have reached the end of the grass and bunchberries and lupine. Gun-metal blue rock thrusts out at us, loose jagged chunks breaking off in our hands and clattering down, making no echoes – all sound is swallowed and smothered by the mist. And now there are fewer cries of "Hawka!" Harsh breathing. Pounding noises of my heart as though it had moved up into my skull and was humping my brain. Flaming pains in thighs and calves and across the chest, whole body going numb, bare hands hanging like hooks, frozen from the wind and grabbing at stones. Oh, to lie here in the immense green mattress, half-smothered in the Earth, buoyed up in the Earth, rocked in the Earth. Lying at this angle, with my feet pointed up toward the blue cliffs where Bohlen, Darnell, and Fineberg clamber on, ghostly mist-men like spiders on a dark web straight above me – or below me – or opposite me – I am on a planet spinning through the universe. Down or up? What does it matter? The wind is rising every minute, becoming a gale – maybe a williwaw! And even though I am exhausted and half-numb from climbing and chilled right to the bone from rolling in the wet grass, *I'm starting to get a hard-on.* I actually want to sink my poor tender prick into this mushy vagina-like stewpot of Earth. I part the moss, digging my fingers down into the wet brown interior – and look! A hidden universe of spiders and ants and caterpillars and worms and slugs, a whole throbbing world. A non-human civilization, where incredible battles take place. Magnificent tumult, drama, action! Will that spider poised among the intertwining roots get the ant-like creature zigzagging in nervous spurts through the dark mass of moss and lichen and roots and grass?

I push deeper into the real underworld, each layer a whole new universe, and Moore kneels beside me – Moore, who has studied the ecology of animals, plants and forests, as well as plant and animal genetics, biochemistry, physiology, and morphology. Moore, who guides me down through the unfolding universes within the breast-soft slopes of Akutan Mountain, the perfect setting for the ultimate lecture on ecology. Simmons gets down on his knees with us. Then Thurston, then Fineberg, then everyone else. We lie at crazy angles, gently probing the tender green flesh, understanding how *this* life form is related to *that* life form and how that tiny weird creature over there could not

Moore.

survive without *those* bits on *that* plant, which makes *this* substance out of *that*. The links between living things flow through endless phases and changes, and the links are never broken. In a leaping flash of Group Mind understanding, we all connect with the idea that all life is interwoven, including us. We are all one. It is pure Zen thought coming out of pure Western technological thought – ecology is just the latest surge of science. For one moment, East and West come into phase, the great dichotomies breaking down, the void coming alive like an all-creating flame.

"If you can relate back far enough," someone says, "I mean ten thousand or a million years, sooner or later you come to the point where the whole bunch of us here had the same father."

"And if you want to push it even further, like maybe a billion years, you come to the point where we hadn't evolved from apes yet, the apes hadn't evolved from the lizards or whatever, the lizards hadn't evolved from the fish, the fish hadn't evolved out of the protoplasm, and for sure you come to the point where all of us – the fish, the lizards, the apes, the bunch of us – we all had the same glob of protoplasm for a daddy."

"Yeah, right, *right!* And, man, can you dig it? It's not just us and the fish and the lizards and all those. Don't forget the birds and the trees and the cactuses and rosebushes! Like, we *all* had the same daddy – the first cell to evolve out of gases floating around the planet."

"So that means –"

And four or five of us scream it out: *"A flower is your brother!"*

There is the ultimate message of ecology – we're all related. Up the last cliff-face of Akutan Mountain we stumble and claw, wild with a burning inspiration, a lightning flash of clarity that transforms the root of thought.

One by one we crawl up over the last ledge, only to find our faces slashed and tears ripped from our eyes by a pounding wind that must be blowing eighty miles an hour across the flat plateau. Twisting mists all around, absolute nothingness. This wind can scoop us up and fling us away into the void. Bohlen's voice, barely audible over the witch cries: "Hey, this must be a williwaw!"

Williwaw, who haunts our minds more profoundly than Cannikin. Williwaw, the wind wraith who stalks the Aleutians. Williwaw, who tears a wheelhouse from a boat as if it were ripping a man's head from his shoulders. Radiation is hypothetical. Wind is a beast making a grab for you. It is our first encounter with the williwaw, though our eyes have roved over the crags as though we might see a giant dervish squinting down at us like a stalking wind lion. We crept through these islands, tense and helpless, the boat limping along under us, Moore saying things like: "Nice williwaw. Good williwaw. Nice boy. Lie down and stay there, boy. Good boy. Good old friendly Willy Williwaw." And now, at the top of Akutan Mountain, who should come raging at us like a ghost out of the mists?

You can lean into an eighty-mile-an-hour wind and it will hold you up as though you were floating, your only connection to the Earth the tips of your rubber boots dug into the loose volcanic gravel. It is the closest thing to flying. But on top of a plateau forty feet wide, surrounded by cliffs and fog, not even a root or a branch to hang on to, it can be terrifying. At any moment the wind might burst just a little more violently and your body will lose its toehold in the skittering gravel and you will be flying for real, out over the edge of the plateau, out and out, and finally down through grey universes until – *crunk-shhhh-riiiiiippppppppp-pulp-slap-skrak.*

But in the Group Mind, we know that if we can't hang on to anything else, we'll hang on to each other's splayed legs. The wind plasters our clothes to us so hard we can see the outlines of each other's bones, and our green jackets billow out on the other side so that we look like inflated toys, or astronauts on the moon, bounding in slow motion, in huge leaps, across chunks of black rock. All this time we have perceived ourselves as anti-heroes of technology, anti-spacemen. The old hippie-beaded rust-stained *Phyllis Cormack*, plowing across vast distances at nine knots, was the perfect anti-spaceship. And now here we are, crazy mirror images of astronauts – princes of the Whole Earth instead of the Megamachine, all hair and comic-book madness. None of this five, four, three, two, one, zero, blast-off shit for us. We are on our way to the Other Moon – Amchitka. The moon landing in 1969 connected technology to metaphysics and gave us a symbol of magic. By landing on Amchitka, the symbol of the other face of technology – waste-maker and ruin-bringer, poisoner of beautiful worlds – we may yet bring people's minds back from dreams of conquering the universe to the reality of the world going to wrack and ruin around them. An ecological Iwo Jima! A landing on the other moon! Scott arriving at a crazy sociopolitical magnetic pole! Leaping slowly and mysteriously as though in one-sixth gravity, half-birds, half-spacemen, we set to work building a cairn. We have not thought to bring the Greenpeace flag, so we pile the biggest loose rocks we can find into an ecology symbol, then a peace symbol, each of them about ten feet wide. The eco-cairn on Akutan. Keziere takes photos of the (historic and/or meaningless) event.

Then quick, before this mad wind really does grab one of us or the lot of us and hurl us into the void, we clamber back to the ledge. But where on the ledge did we climb over? And what if we start down the wrong side? We could find ourselves on the face of a hundred-foot sheer cliff. "Help!" yells Moore. "Where am I?" yells Thurston. "This way!" yells Bohlen. *Hawkaaaaaaa!*

And down over the ledge we go, rocks plinking and shattering as we kick them loose, but we are not afraid. One of the powers of the Group Mind is to foresee disaster – or so we think, madly, caught up in the euphoria of the day. Nobody falls or gets smashed on the head or even scratched. Everyone is in one piece when we reach the meadows. We are in the lee of the mountains. Perhaps a williwaw still rages back up at the top, but we are inland now, and the wind is a low moan and a flapping of the grasses. Silence unfolds from the mist-lands and the world around us is wet Greenpeace green again, a land that seems never to have been touched by man. At any moment a grazing dinosaur might shuffle heavily from around a hill.

Finally I am by myself, sagged against a blue-black outcropping of rock, numb fingers fumbling through jacket pockets for my log book, and fumbling hours longer, it seems, to find a pencil, mind flipping around wildly for some handle, some key word or phrase that will hold the magic of what has just happened. Later, when I am back to "normal" – no longer a free-flying eco-freak in an epiphany – I will flip open the log book and there it will be, the Diamond of Wisdom, the Final Truth, the Sacred Rune of Akutan, the Absolute Summary of Everything. And it comes. One moment my head is full of swirling ecstasy and planet love, and the next moment, in the rain and cold, fumbling like a bear with a ballpoint, I write down my key to the miraculous day:

> PARANOID GRANDIOSITY
> IS THE HUMAN
> SOUL

THURSDAY, SEPTEMBER 30, 1971

In the afternoon we get ready to take leave of Akutan. There is still no word on when the bomb will go off, but the most consistent reports place the date sometime between mid-October and early November. Which means we still have two to four weeks to kill – unless Richard Nixon suddenly makes himself perfectly clear. After about a dozen meetings in the galley, we decide that the best bet is to inch our way up the chain, closing in on our prey as slowly as possible. Cannikin has proven elusive, but that just means we must stalk all the harder. Darnell has instituted a no-eating-between-meals policy to slow the rate at which we're gobbling up our supplies, we've bought up all the goods we can at the grocery store – not much, but maybe enough – and Cormack is planning to replenish the water tanks at the abandoned whaling station across the bay. Simmons and Metcalfe have gone ashore for the last time to get a message through to U.S. Customs and Immigration in Anchorage, advising them that we will be taking a "deep-sea" route to Atka, an island several hundred miles closer to Amchitka. We assume that permission will come through within twenty-four hours and we'll be able to leave Akutan. The deep-sea route allows us to bypass Atka and sneak up on Amchitka, circle the island and scout out the territory, then fall back to Atka and hang on there. From Atka it will be an easier run. The weather is getting rougher every day, and the closer we are when the test date is finally announced, the less likely we are to be stopped by storms.

When Simmons and Metcalfe return to the *Greenpeace*, everybody is getting ready for supper. Cormack is up in the radio room, flipping through some maps, a grizzle of white hair starting to grow like a mat on his face – "Seeing's how all you *pro*-fessors and *re*-porters've got beards, thought I'd try one on for size. 'Course it'll be a man's beard, not like that stringy thing on that Thurston fella." Idly, Cormack looks up, and sees a flash of metal and foam out in the ocean beyond the bay. "Coast Guard cutter's coming," he says, in that matter-of-fact way of his, in exactly the same tone of voice as he'd said, a week ago, "Test's been delayed." If the Second Coming was announced, he'd come tromping in here and say, "God's coming." If the planet's biosphere finally collapsed: "Sky's falling." Or (this one I have imagined a dozen times): "Boat's sinking."

Our long-awaited moment of confrontation with the American Empire has finally arrived. The hassles between Metcalfe, Simmons, and Fineberg all the way across the Gulf centred on: what can they do to stop us? We are a Canadian boat in international waters, yet only three miles away from Amchitka, Ground Zero, around which there is a fifty-mile security zone. What can the Americans do to stop us, short of an act of piracy, or a reversion to the time-honoured naval tradition of blasting us out of the water with their cannons? Cannikin is a key component in the building of the Anti-Ballistic Missile System, which is itself a step in the direction of Dr Strangelove's famous bummer. Caught between the wish not to fuck up what little remains of her tattered alliances, and an obsession with the old nuclear deterrent fantasy, America might bust a gut over this one. They can't win. If they do nothing, we'll concentrate public attention on the recklessness of the test just by parking so dangerously close and risking our lives. If they blow their cool and grab us, we'll become the subject of an international incident with far-reaching consequences. At the very least we will be a flaming match dropping into the dry hay of Canadian nationalism. Politics, politics, politics.

I crash down the ladder into the galley, rapping at everybody in a tense, excited voice. "John says Coast Guard cutter's coming." And at that moment the question comes into focus in my mind: Saaaaaay, how come we're not out in international waters? This wasn't supposed to happen 100 yards off the shore of Akutan, an American island. We must be *inside* their territorial limit, where our diplomatic immunity or whatever doesn't apply. But we heard what Cormack said. We can't stay out in the open for a whole month, not in the October storms. There's a fine jittery air in the boat. Nobody's overreacting. We're all keeping a pretty good surface cool. Then again, four times I find myself going from the poop deck back to my bunk to get my pen and log book, and four times I forget what I wanted by the time I get there, then hurry back outside to watch the approach of the cutter and suddenly remember that I still don't have my pen and log book. Wanting to get all the details down. What time is it, *exactly*? What direction is she coming from? What's the date?

Our only weapons are our tape recorders and typewriters and notebooks and cameras. Which give us access to the mass media in Canada, the Office of the Prime Minister, and our public support – *as long as we remain in clear view*. Everything depends on that. If nobody knows we are out here, the Yanks can do anything they want. No non-American in the world today can watch the approach of one of the symbols of America's might without a slight case of nerves. Metcalfe's hand shakes with excitement as he fumbles through the boxes by his bunk for his film and tapes. Keziere mutters about what a rotten time of day this has happened, getting dark, available light going fast. He tries on one lens after another, darting in and out of the galley to check his light readings. Fineberg arranges his papers neatly on his clipboard, flicking his ballpoint around like a cowboy checking his pistol. Several hummed snatches of "We Love You, Greenpeace," some actual giggling – and then, suddenly, the engine starts up.

What? Birmingham has pulled up the anchor, Cormack is heaving his huge bulk up from the engine room and tromping up to the Penthouse, yelling orders at Birmingham, spinning the wheel around. The engine is throbbing and clunking, water is gurgling up at the stern, and, my God, *the fucking boat is moving*. Thurston throws up his hands in despair as Bohlen and Metcalfe, already at the bridge, demand to know what the hell Cormack thinks he's doing. Cormack is slamming gears around, spinning the wheel, waving his arms, and yelling at Birmingham, and the *Greenpeace* is heaving around, engine throttling up. Are we making a run for it? Cummings tries for the sixth time to light his pipe.

"Think maybe old Cormack's flipped out?" I ask.

Fineberg.

"Maybe," he says.

Bohlen comes down from the bridge, shrugging and shaking his head, on the verge of laughing or crying, I don't know which. He reports that Cormack is in one of those moods again. That means he's bustling around like a bull, and if you try to talk to him he'll just tell you to shut up or get the hell out of the way or fuck off. All the Greenhawks can do is collapse into a collective state of sitting back to watch what happens. The Coast Guard vessel slows down. "What next?" Keziere chuckles helplessly. Then a sudden blast of smoke from the cutter's stack as the crew catch on. It's absurd – we seem to be under full throttle, which only amounts to nine or ten knots, and that big mother of a Coast Guard ship can probably do thirty knots. They're coming in through the mouth of the bay. Maybe a wily old sea fox like Captain John can dodge around them and beat it out to sea. He can't just go forward – the bay's a dead end and we're trapped. Even if we do manage to dart through their fingers, they'll get us out in the open, or send the Hercules after us again. It's no use, John! We can't escape! Why are we trying?

Then, as abruptly as it started up, the engine stops. Cormack is yelling at Birmingham to let down the anchor. We have moved about half a mile up the bay.

"So this's what's next," says Keziere, gurgling in quiet hysteria. "We start up for no reason. And then we stop for no reason. It figures. Fuck *around*."

Bohlen's got the binoculars. "Have they got a gun?" I ask him.

"Oh yes, sure. Ah, I can see the name. The *Confidence*."

"Well, they can afford to be confident. What kind of a gun is it?"

"Dunno. It's covered up."

"Thank Christ for that."

"No need to worry," says Fineberg. "I advised the CIA in my last secret report that you guys would give up without a fight. We won't shoot you."

One thing about Fineberg, he does manage to get in some licks while the blows are landing all around him. The shaft is so perfect, it is a shame Darnell and I are the only ones close enough to hear it. Fineberg is still feeling hurt that anyone would suspect him of being a CIA agent – he, Dick Fineberg, who has been fighting the military-industrial complex through his whole academic career, who turned down a juicy postdoctoral grant so that he can risk his life trying to bring the bastards down and generally give peace a chance, who has draped a sweatshirt carelessly over the licence plate on his motorcycle to protect Taiwanese people from the criminal charge of entertaining foreign visitors. He is accused of academic nit-picking when he points out that we have fallen victim to paranoid grandiosity because we lack clarity of purpose. Just before we got boarded by the *Confidence* at Akutan, for instance, Metcalfe claimed with existential grandiosity that for the *Greenpeace*, "the action transcends the law because it's a whole new movie, a new scenario, a new plot."

And now, here we stand on the old squeaky greasy wooden planks of the *Phyllis Cormack* in Akutan Bay, watching John Wayne's boys bearing down on us in their immense armed super-dreadnaught.

"I guess this part's real," I say to Thurston.

"Another grand piano, man," he says.

He looks out over the Surf-Cloud, the peak with the eco-cairn, the lovely cut of the wind across the water. *This whole scene is a grand piano.* He is totally alive, alert to every nuance of the situation, so turned on to so many levels of reality, always looking out in a way that the rest of us look only occasionally, seeing the world as a never-ending treasure, and life itself as a constant state of grace. He stands absolutely still on the poop deck, absorbing the flavour of the experience, then drifts into the galley with Darnell, who yells back to the rest of us, "Come on. Might as well have supper. It'll be a while before they get to us." Darnell is almost unflappable, the stereotypical stoic Canadian who doesn't say much, just does things quietly and heroically, and in the end he gets killed and the American or Englishman gets the girl. Well, sure. Why not have supper? I'm hungry, come to think of it.

"We really are Hobbits," says Moore, chuckling to himself as we troop in and sit down around the galley table. We even break out a final stashed-away bottle of rum.

"Christ," says Metcalfe, "we can't go to Amchitka now. We won't have anything left to drink when the fucking bomb goes off."

Darnell has the turkey out of the oven, Metcalfe pours rum into china mugs, the naked bulb in the ceiling makes it very bright and cozy in the tiny white enamel-walled galley, and we pretend to be unbothered by what's going on out in the gathering blue dark. We've thought up a thousand schemes for dealing with the Yanks when the moment of the bust comes – hitting them with wet mops, throwing roles of toilet paper at them, peeing on them from the upper deck, fighting them off with grappling hooks, taking off all our clothes and lining up at attention on the poop deck and singing, "We Love You, Greenpeace," and everything in between. But these scenarios were built on the old high-seas immunity theory. As it is, we're caught with our pants down inside their waters.

"When they come in and start poking their sten guns at us," says Metcalfe, "we burst out singing 'The Star-Spangled Banner' and demand political asylum from Canada."

"Yeah, the whole thing was an elaborate trick to escape from Trudeau's Communist slave state, right?"

"And then we sell our stories to *Life*, and Keziere sells his photos of the first Canadian refugees to arrive in the United States of America from north of the border, and then –"

"We retire to Morocco and smoke hash for the rest of our lives."

"And Canada claims that we're actually prisoners of war and uses us as pawns in a defence-sharing agreement with Russia."

"And the Royal Canadian Air Force sends a Piper Cub loaded with tennis balls over the White House and drops them all."

"And the U.S. government immediately surrenders –"

"And once again we save the universe!"

It is a terrific supper. Halfway through, we spot a motor launch bobbing across the water toward us from the *Confidence*, which has stopped about half a mile away. Four figures are clearly to be seen *standing up* in the launch. Standing up! It must be some crazy navy boarding tradition – the water is rough enough that any sane man would be huddled down in the boat. The launch cuts across our bow and comes puttering up to the poop deck on the starboard – no, port. At the last minute our collective cool breaks down and Keziere, Bohlen, Metcalfe, and Simmons all rush outside. The skipper waits up in the Penthouse, one hand on the wheel, the other in his pants pocket, one leg folded across the other, his fedora low on his forehead, looking like a pleasure boater curiously watching the approach of another boat – might be peddling shrimp for all he knows.

Birmingham comes crashing into the galley and points at the poster of Nixon, whose nose has been festooned with two darts – two *green* darts – ever since the night we heard about the test being delayed. "Gotta take that down," says Birmingham. I remember that the MANGE D'LA MARDE poster came down when we were out on the Gulf because we kept getting thrown against it and it was starting to tear. I go and get it out from where somebody stashed it under a bunk, and when I get back, Birmingham has pulled down the Nixon poster. "It's no laughing matter," he says – genuinely angry, I think – as Moore, Thurston, Darnell, and Fineberg howl and pound their fists with glee. Birmingham's normally super-white skin is turning pink. "No laughing matter at all. You damn young smart alecks can laugh all you want, but just you remember we're in their water right now, and we're in enough trouble as it is without going and getting them madder at us. How'd you like it if you went on an American ship and saw a picture of our Prime Minister with a couple of darts on his face?" Explosion of redoubled laughter, Moore and Thurston gasping for air. Wow, when Dave Birmingham gets mad, it's really a trip. The docile, polite, 'scuse-me-for-butting-in-I-know-it's-none-of-my-business Birmingham – ten times as strong as any one aboard except Cormack, and maybe the stolid Darnell – is almost shaking with fury. He shoves past me on his way into the Opium Den to hide the poster, not noticing MANGE D'LA MARDE rolled up in my hand. Immediately I tack it up in place of Nixon.

We are still lying back against the galley walls laughing our heads off when Bohlen comes bounding and whooping through the galley door, his eyebrows halfway up to his hairline, yelling, "*Whoooopppiiieeee!* Listen to this!" He's reading aloud from a cablegram-looking piece of paper, in a jabbering delirious-with-joy voice: "Due to the situation we are in, we crew of the *Confidence* feel that what you are doing is for the good of all mankind. If our hands weren't tied by these military bonds, we would be in the same position you are in if it was at all possible. Good luck. We are behind you one hundred percent."

"*What's going on?*" screams Thurston. "You mean they're not busting us?"

"You mean they're on *our* side?"

"The U.S. Coast Guard is on *our* side?"

Wildly, the thought flashes through my mind that maybe, while we've been out of radio contact, the Revolution has happened in America and it's all over, and the revolutionaries are coming out to let us know there's nothing to worry about, there won't be any H-bomb test at Amchitka. Peace, love, and freedom have conquered and Nixon is locked away. Now, having switched instantly from hysterical helpless laughter to heart-pumping adrenaline excitement, we jam our way through the galley door and out on deck. It takes a while for our eyes to adjust to the gloom, but there, tied to the *Greenpeace* with a rope, is the

DUE TO THE SITUATION WE ARE IN WE THE CREW OF THE CONFIDENCE FEEL THAT
WHAT YOU ARE DOING IS FOR THE GOOD OF ALL MANKIND. IF OUR HANDS WEREN'T
TIED BY THESE MILITARY BONDS, WE WOULD BE IN THE SAME POSITION YOU ARE IN
IF IT WERE AT ALL POSSIBLE.

GOOD LUCK WE ARE BEHIND YOU 100%

The letter from the crew of the U.S. Coast Guard vessel *Confidence*.

Coast Guard launch, about a third the size of our whole boat. It bobs there with three young guys standing in it – frogmen? Yeah, they're wearing wetsuits, but without flippers or goggles or helmets, just navy wool caps on their heads. Metcalfe jabs his microphone at them, yelling: "Is it okay with you guys if we get this on the eleven o'clock news?" He steps back with his National Film Board camera on his shoulder and the other hand still holding out the tape recorder mike. Bohlen stands beside the launch with the three frogmen bobbing around behind him, reading the message aloud – *get it on the record*. Keziere leaps around with his camera. Cummings peeks over Bohlen's shoulder, scribbling furiously in his notebook, and Moore, Thurston, and I are drawn to the action like iron filings to a magnet. I have only to take one look at the Coast Guard guys to see that – my God, they're *freaks!* One of them is a chubby guy, a Fabulous Furry Freak Brother. Another is a black guy. I throw my hand out to him and we automatically engage in the revolutionary handshake, which I used to think was silly but which now makes perfect sense. It is a hell of a fine feeling to be gripping that American's hand. They have not had to look too closely at us to see that not a few of us have "freak" stamped all over our faces, our hair, our clothes, what we're doing. The vibes! It is a near-instantaneous telepathic communication. The enemy is dying from within! The enemy has a revolution on his hands! The mere physical barriers between races and cultures collapse before the wave of evolutionary mutation. A new race is in the making. The freaks on the *Greenpeace* meet the freaks on the U.S. Coast Guard cutter *Confidence* like two small bands of *Homo sapiens* rushing with cries of recognition into a joyous embrace, while the Neanderthals, a strange brutish shambling race of turned-off hung-up blind grotesque primitives, haunt the world around us. Brotherhood is powerful. "Brother, am I glad to see you! Man, we were expecting a pack of, you know, Green Berets, to come leaping down on us. Seeing you freaks is like seeing angels, man!" The black guy and the Freak

Commander Floyd Hunter of the *Confidence* pays a visit to the *Greenpeace*.

Brother guy are rapping madly away. The third dude comes on much more cool and got-it-together, as if to say, "Everything's out of sight, man. You know, the whole scene is so mind-blowing every day that it's just . . . wow . . . far out . . . I mean, either you can dig it or you can't. This's a gas, man. Let's all dig it."

Meanwhile, as this good contact high unfolds between us on the poop deck, old Captain John is having the book thrown at him by the Commander of the *Confidence*, and the Revolution in America is a hell of a long way from over. Though I didn't even notice him coming aboard, the Commander is doing what we expected all along – busting the *Greenpeace*. My research tells me that he was very cool when he climbed aboard. None of that stereotyped snappy military clown stuff. He has his role, and the range of his actions is defined in ink. Well, he is a U.S. Coast Guard commander. He has a good presence, even if he moves like a robot and his shaved head looks as though it just came out of the head-making machine. The electrodes have been peeled off, the eyelids have been tested and found to be in working condition, the ego component has been installed and the switch thrown to ON. All that remains is for the head to be attached to the filament-wound glass epoxy android body unit, and voila! – Commander Floyd Hunter, Serial Number 774-8888-002, Model #37. Function: Officer in charge of U.S. Coast Guard vessel *Confidence*, 17th District, U.S. Coast Guard Command. Instructions for use: Feed required tape (C-90 microminiaturized psychotronic cassettes now available) at specified psi-band into molecular ether-sensitive ego component. Results guaranteed! Which is to say that Commander Hunter doesn't look like any relative of mine. He wears a wetsuit with a garment that resembles a pilot's nylon jumpsuit over it, a rather quaint navy blue turtleneck sweater, an orange life jacket fastened neatly over top of all that – presumably in strict accordance with some subsection of some rule on officers' attire in some regulations handbook. He stands in the Penthouse with the air of an honest but world-weary highway patrolman talking to the driver of the car he's just pulled over, informing the master of CAN VES GREEN PEACE, Captain John C. Cormack of Vancouver, that he has just broken the law, and he is liable to have his vessel impounded.

But there is an aura of irony about Commander Hunter. He may know his role and conform to it perfectly, yet he retains a sense of himself that is quite separate from the situation and the role into which he has been thrust. Like having formally to board this rather lovely, almost antique-looking fishing boat skippered by one of those crazy but delightful, even honourable (in their own knavish way) old captains, famous along the Northwest Coast for their exploits. Yeah, the Commander of the *Confidence* seems basically a good man with an eye for the texture of a situation, a sense of himself, and a sense of humour.

While the freak convention takes place out on deck, Commander Hunter reads out a warrant for our arrest. He then hands a piece of paper to Cormack and the two of them go down to the galley, where Bohlen and Metcalfe introduce themselves, Bohlen as one of the executives of the Don't Make a Wave Committee, the Canadian group that chartered Captain Cormack's vessel and whose instructions he has been following, etc., etc. All very formal, all very stiff, with a shivery air of excitement and humour and a shared recognition of the real political import of the scene. Yet in another way, the formalities are silly. We are human beings, members of the same society. These men are practically cousins and this is a family squabble. A polite and proper exchange is taking place between two men who might otherwise be sitting down at the bar to have a drink together. While Commander Hunter is formally charging Captain Cormack with a "customs violation," their crewmen are shaking hands and exchanging messages of support and sharing the last of the rum. We are ecstatic, joyous, amused, angry, frightened, frustrated, calm, cool, crazy, sane, together, unnerved, overwhelmed, happy, sad, content, edgy, and jittery all at once. Commander Hunter lays the piece of paper on the galley table and flips out his notebook and ballpoint, at the same moment as Metcalfe flips out his notebook and ballpoint.

STATEMENT OF CUSTOMS VIOLATION, F/V PHYLLIS CORMACK/GREENPEACE.

    I. SITUATION

    A. PHYLLIS CORMACK ARRIVED AKUTAN ON 26 SEP HAVING GIVEN COAST GUARD REQUIRED ADVANCE NOTICE OF ARRIVAL. VSL DID NOT REPORT HER ARRIVAL TO CUSTOMS WITHIN 24 HOURS AS REQUIRED BY 19 USC 1433 AND DID NOT MAKE FORMAL ENTRY WITH CUSTOMS WITHIN 48 HOURS AS REQUIRED BY 19 USC 1435. VSL HAS NOT TO THIS TIME NOTIFIED CUSTOMS.

    B. DISTRICT DIRECTOR OF CUSTOMS HAS ASKED COAST GUARD TO NOTIFY MASTER OF PHYLLIS CORMACK THAT HE HAS INCURRED PENALTY WITHIN U.S. CUSTOMS FOR FAILURE TO REPORT UNDER THE TARIFF ACT OF 1932 (19 USC 1435). LETTER OF PENALTY WILL BE SENT TO HOME ADDRESS OF MASTER. CUSTOMS HAS ALSO REQUESTED COAST GUARD TO NOTIFY MASTER OF THE REQUIREMENTS OF THE TARIFF ACT OF 1932. 19 USC 1436 PROVIDES THAT VSLS FOUND IN VIOLATION OF 19 USC 1435 ARE LIABLE FOR A FINE OF UP TO 1,000 DOLLARS.

    C. IF VESSEL DOES NOT MAKE FORMAL ENTRY TO CUSTOMS BEFORE HE DEPARTS AKUTAN HE WILL BE IN VIOLATION OF 19 USC 1585, FOR WHICH PENALTY IS UP TO 5,000 DOLLARS FINE AND/OR FORFEITURE OF VESSEL.

    2. ACTION:

ENTRY WITH CUSTOMS MAY BE MADE BY GREENPEACE

OR HER REPRESENTATIVE CONTACTING THE DISTRICT
DIRECTOR OF CUSTOMS IN ANCHORAGE TO REQUEST A
FORMAL ENTRY INTO A NON-CUSTOMS PORT. . . .
PHYLLIS CORMACK MUST ARRANGE FOR A CUSTOMS
OFFICER TO PROCEED TO AKUTAN TO MAKE FORMAL ENTRY.

The gist of this tight-assed message is that we blew it by crossing the border without reporting to customs. All our elaborate planning to be in international waters has come to nothing. They have us. And what now? End of the attack on the weapons makers of Amchitka. End of the Fellowship of the Piston Rings. Go home, Hobbits. The Dark Lord wins. Custer drives off the Indians with a wave of his hand – they forgot to pay their entry fee to the Little Big Horn Theatre. Game ball. Or is it?

The freak convention is coming to an end and we want to give our brothers some gifts. Over the side go the presents. We find the Nixon poster and hand it over, along with the green darts, a handful of books on eco-tactics, a small Canadian flag, some peace pennants, Canadian cigarettes, and a copy of *The Female Eunuch*. It is all we can spare. They especially dig the poster – "That'll go up for sure, man" – and the darts. They tell us how they have come to be handing us a message of support while they are busting us. There is a year-long waiting list to get in the Coast Guard, and if you get in, you don't have to go to Vietnam. "It's a four-year stint, and it's a drag – it's really a drag – but you get back home alive, you know?" They first got word about the *Greenpeace* mission three or four months ago. "But the brass are hip. They know what's coming down. When we set out on this little caper they didn't tell us anything about where we were going or what we were up to. You know? And that's weird. Usually they don't give a shit and everybody pretty well knows what's happening. But this time – not a word, man. Just keep us all in the fog. Wasn't till a couple of hours ago word sneaked out it was you guys we were going to bust." They got their petition together immediately and started getting guys to sign it. At that time no one knew who was going to be taking the brass to the *Greenpeace*, but everybody wanted to sign. At the last minute, men were fighting to grab the petition and sign it. "Sure hope you guys can squeeze outta this and get on up there and shove it up their asses. So – do it, man. Far out."

Well, now. This is getting incredible. The radio message from the *Camsell*, Lucy and Daisy Sewid's similar greeting on behalf of the Kwak'waka'wakw people, the United Church of Canada, and some fifty other organizations ranging from the B.C. Federation of Labour to the Liberal Party of Canada speaking through the Prime Minister. This is great. But if all these people care so much, how come they are all carrying on busily doing what they always do? Why is business going on as usual? In a sickening flash that takes me as low as I was high a moment before, I see that a revolution can go no faster or further than people themselves, and together people generate inertia. Even in this situation, when hundreds of thousands of people all over the political spectrum join together in a common objection, there is not enough momentum to move people out of the mass inertia. The Megamachine continues to plunge unimpeded toward destruction. These guys in the Coast Guard have taken a huge step – in effect, they have committed an act of treason. In a different age they might have been court martialled, or shot. But their strength lies in the fact that all of them were willing to commit the act of defiance. And yet between us, even with all the support we have – in Canada, the closest thing to a mass movement in decades, and for the Coast Guard rebels, the peace and Black Liberation movements – damn it, we still aren't strong enough to throw the androids down. They are still running the show. The Coast Guard freaks had to wait for the Commander to turn his back and then sneak their message to us.

Now, at the moment when Commander Hunter stands up in the

Metcalfe, Bohlen, and Fineberg.

galley, Cummings rushes back to warn the crewmen, who hand back the rum, stash their books and pennants in their wetsuits, and come to attention. Fully occupying his role, the Commander walks across the poop deck and climbs into the launch. He must notice that one of his men has a Canadian flag tucked in his belt and that their wetsuits are bulky with goodies, but he neither blinks nor not-blinks. As well, he could not have failed to note in a single glance that the crew of the *Greenpeace* are not all of the same mould. Some obvious regular citizens are aboard – Metcalfe, Bohlen, Cormack, and Birmingham – but there are also some characters who look a lot like hippies. No reaction has been prescribed in the prerecorded instructions, so no reaction is made. He stares evenly into Keziere's Leica and Metcalfe's purring NFB camera, accustomed to being in the presence of the media and giving no hint of his private thoughts.

In spite of the fact that the Commander's role appears to have taken him over completely, I still pick up that vaguely warm sense of humour. "Will we be seeing you again?" I ask him. He flashes the thinnest tic of a smile and says, "You can count on it."

The launch bearing Commander Hunter heads back through the thickening darkness, the three freaks flashing v-signs and grins at us whenever the Commander isn't looking. Finally the launch vanishes into the steel grey bulk of the *Confidence*, which stays where it is, looking suspiciously as though it is blockading the mouth of the bay. "Well, we're in a splendid trap now, aren't we?" mutters Thurston, still shaking his head in amazement at the many flaming extremes of the last half-hour. Yeah. We are in a trap, no doubt about it. Amchitka is slipping out of reach. First the delay, and now this. Up until now, the faith has burned in me. We *will* make it. Our vibes are so good, we are in harmony with so many forces, magic is afoot. We'll make it for sure. But now. . . . Well, there sits the *Confidence*, curled up like a cat with a hundred eyes.

But they are being careful to play it very neatly. A boat in an allied country that has been blessed by church and state alike can only be dealt with diplomatically. By arresting us, they took the chance that even more attention will be drawn to us and to the protest. And that's exactly what happens. Metcalfe gets the story on the eleven o'clock news. It goes national in Canada and makes the front pages in Toronto, Washington, and Alaska, and – good grief – we are even briefly noted in the New York City press. Not because we were busted, but because a whole boatload of Coast Guard guys supported a protest action undertaken against their own government by a foreign power. What? Is there some kind of mutiny brewing in the Coast Guard? Once again, it was either our karma running or our blind luck. Out of the jaws of a boo-boo we had snatched a public relations victory.

Simmons and Fineberg have "I told you so" written all over their faces. We have been caught on a technicality, just the sort of thing they were trying to warn us about. And yet . . . and yet. . . . Maybe this is the best thing that could have happened. Without the confrontation, we might have petered out quietly here among the islands, waiting and waiting and waiting for the test. They delayed it once. They can delay it again. Certainly they can keep it up longer than we can. Sooner or later we will run out of food or water or energy or will or spirit, whichever goes first, and we'll have to turn around and head home. But now we won't have to go quietly. Now we are making some waves. Whatever damage the brass inflicted on us, it is already backfiring on them. Instead of leaving us alone to sink into obscurity, they have confronted us and got us onto the front page. Even Simmons and Fineberg can see that the situation is still in a state of flux. Will it continue to work more to our advantage than to theirs? Who can declare with certainty that we are blessed or cursed, star-crossed or enchanted?

That has been the question since early in the voyage. Three days out of Vancouver, Birmingham came up from the engine room and announced that he was resigning as engineer. Now that he'd had a chance to examine the engine, he wasn't willing to take responsibility for it. He would stay on as the Captain's assistant, but that was all. "This boat," he said, "runs on no known principles of science or engineering. It runs on shithouse luck."

And as we crossed the Gulf of Alaska, most of us throwing up or frozen in fear as the mountain-size swells heaved toward us, Cormack kept shaking his head in amazement, scratching his chin, and muttering, "Can't figure it out. Never seen the weather so calm out here this time of year. Should be blowing like a bastard and here she is, flat calm."

"It's our karma, John," Thurston explained.

"Huh," said Cormack. "Crazy weather."

"No," Thurston insisted, "it's our *vibes*, John. We've got good vibes. That means good karma. Don't worry, we'll be all right."

Who knows the difference between good karma and shithouse luck, and who cares? As long as it keeps working. Even now, although we have sustained two body blows, each strong enough by itself to wipe us out – the delay and the bust – we are still in motion and gradually we are bringing more and more pressure to bear. Around the same time Birmingham abdicated as guardian of the engine, a radio message came in from the icebreaker *Camsell:* "You have our full support for your courageous and idealistic action. Wish we could do more to help but we can only pray and hope that the test will be cancelled." The lightning rod flares through the electronic night of the Global Village – twice hit, the *Greenpeace* looms larger than ever when it should be sinking. With every delay, every fuck-up, more public attention is turned toward the protest. To the Americans we are still a tiny symbol, scarcely a spark. But there is tinder everywhere. Ah, we *are* Hobbits! In the Great War of the Rings, the Hobbits were too small and weak to make much difference in the battles that raged on the Field of Cormallen outside the gates of the Kingdom of the Dark Lord. Their humble function was to sneak in through the back door of Mordor and hurl the One Ring into the fire. Like the Hobbits, we have no great swords to draw. We have no magic power. We will only be the temporary Bearers of the One Ring, while the real struggle is carried by a mass alliance of Black warriors and white warriors and wizards of legal magic, environmental organizations, anti-war groups, troops of Quakers and other pacifists, and legions of elf-like flower children.

It is the old shithouse karma at work again – that and Metcalfe's nose for news. He was on the radiophone within minutes of the Coast Guard's departure, feeding the fires of public awareness and unrest. In another stroke of ridiculous luck, we found that the radio, which hadn't been getting through to Vancouver at all, was suddenly loud and clear. In moving the boat, Cormack had accidentally put us in a position where the mountains were no longer in the way.

Friday, October 1, 1971

In the morning the *Confidence* is gone, maybe on another mission or maybe lurking out in Unimak Pass, waiting to counter our next move, whatever that may be. Our range of options is narrow. Metcalfe gets through to the Coast Guard and learns that we don't necessarily have to wait for a customs officer to come to us. We can head back along the Aleutian chain toward the mainland of Alaska, to a place called Sand Point. There we can see a customs officer, clear customs, and maybe wiggle out of the mess we are in, and still be in a position to strike for Amchitka once the date for the test is announced. The risk is that by going into Sand Point, we may be stepping into a deeper pit of red tape and technicalities, but there is not much choice at this stage.

Cormack ups anchor and we head out of Akutan Bay and back through Unimak Pass, past Unimak Island toward the Alaska Peninsula. For the first time, we are heading away from Amchitka. But maybe it is only a temporary setback. If nothing else, we can restock our supplies at Sand Point, and though we will be 300 miles farther from our objective than we had been at Akutan, we will still be within a week's sailing of Amchitka. Given decent weather, we could make it there in time for the rendezvous with Cannikin. There are a lot more ifs, buts, and maybes than before, but we are still in the ball game. Whatever pressure is applied just by our presence is still being applied, only more so. Not only have we succeeded in getting as far as we have – within striking distance – and not only did we accidentally manage to elude the Coast Guard at sea, now we have also triggered a near-mutiny. This morning things do not seem so bad at all. If they pin us down in Sand Point, we can scream and holler and maybe hype the level of action even further. Or make a break for it. Yeah, come to think of it, we still have plenty of options. The battle isn't lost.

Yet as we head down along the south coast of Unimak Island, a wintery wind whipping the waves and a few flakes of snow stinging across the decks, old Cormack comes up to me and says, "Wanna make a bet?"

"Maybe. What's the bet?"

He leans forward, as though to whisper a secret. "I'll bet you that it's the [mumbled word] of the *Greenpeace*."

"The *what* of the *Greenpeace*?"

"Didn't you hear me? Well, I'll say it again, *puh puh puh puh puh*, this's the [mumbled word] of the *Greenpeace*."

"What the hell're you saying, John?"

He grinned, one of those I-know-something-you-don't-know grins of his. "Wal, put it this way, since you can't seem to hear what a fella's telling you. I either said it was the *retreat* of the *Greenpeace* or something else. Now that's the bet. Whaddya think it is?"

"I'd say it's the retreat, John. I don't think we're completely beaten yet."

Thurston, Moore, and Darnell.

"The word I used wasn't retreat, I'll tell you."

"So you think we've had it, John? We're finished?"

"Wal, I didn't say retreat, so I must've said the other word. Even a dummy can figure that out."

For some reason Cormack can't bring himself to say the word out loud – *defeat*. Briefly I wonder if there is some sort of taboo on uttering it, like the taboos against opening cans upside down and hanging up mugs facing the wrong way.

"Why don't you just say it, John? *Defeat*. D, E, F, E, A, T."

He shrugs and looks away. "That's what the bet's about," he said. "Which one is it?"

But he won't say it. Maybe he can't say it. I begin for the first time to understand John Cormack. He has probably never said the word "defeat" aloud in his life. Somewhere in my mind, a warning bell rings. If John can't say "defeat," if he can't cry uncle when the time comes to cry uncle, then he may yet take us to the bottom of the sea out of sheer stubbornness. His word on how safe something is may not be absolutely reliable. A man who cannot admit defeat is a man who will take you over the edge of the world. That makes him a strong man, an indomitable man, a man of iron will. Ah, John!

SATURDAY, OCTOBER 2, 1971

The Bering Sea is behind us. We did not get to know much about its mood, except that it is getting mean, and the ice packs will soon be awakening. Winter is on the wind. The windows in the Penthouse are fogging on the inside and getting covered with cold wet slush on the outside. Coming across the slow mystical back of the Gulf, we gathered often in that little tram-like booth, the centre of daytime social activity. Now it is cold, like one of those old wooden streetcar waiting stations, the kind that were covered with cigarette butts and candy wrappers and old newspapers, stiff gusts of wind blowing through the door every time someone entered. Outside, there is a hum and a wail. The window panes rattle. The old waiting station swings back and forth and bounces along in a movement that can only be described as doggy. We have to wear gloves now, and steam puffs from our mouths. We have to stomp our feet to keep them warm as we alternate between taking the wheel and going out into the sleet and the icy teeth of the wind to wipe the slush off the glass so we can see where we are going. At night the radar is on all the time, but we still have to work at the windows to see the lighthouses and beacons. And now we are in the fishing lanes. Lights move blurrily in the puddles on the windows – halibut boats, crab boats, shrimp boats. Once we pass a Russian trawler. The crew's voices come jabbering through the radio, the powerful generators running their electronic equipment overriding our tiny side-band. "Yep," says Cormack, "them Russian boats has always got the latest stuff." Occasionally, over the woofing whining keening noises that come through the radio, we hear Japanese mariners calling to one another.

It is an odd, lonely corner of the world. We are close to the American mainland, moving between the peninsula and little clusters of islands with names like Poperechnoi, Dolgoi, Ukolnoi, Iliasik, Chernabura, Sanak, and Canton. Between the Japanese and Russian voices, and Cormack on the lookout for other Canadian vessels skippered by men he knows, the area does not feel American. It is completely removed from neon jungles, race riots, Mayor Daly, smog, freeways, billboards, pop art, suburbia, napalm, and all those other distinctly American things. Yet there are names on the charts that tell us clearly enough we are near the shore of the good old U.S.A. To the north, with great white scallops of wind-trimmed cloud around its peaks, looms Pavlof Volcano, yet the shore below it is called Long Beach. After Cape Tolstoi comes Cape Seal, after Belkofski Point comes Bluff Point, north of Unga Spit is Lefthand Bay. Opposite Kaslokan Point lies Kitchen Anchorage. John Rock is only a few thousand yards from Olga Island, and going through Popof Strait you are just north of a bay called Saddler's Mistake. Along the Alaska peninsula itself, no one can quibble with the naming of the peaks, even as the Russian influence wanes: After Pavlof Volcano comes Mount Dana, then Hoodoo Mountain, Monolith Peak, Pyramid Peak, and Cathedral Peak – names that speak to the Arctic timelessness of the place, no signs of civilization at all beyond the remote flickering beacons. The drum-rolling Gulf of Alaska was a whole new world after the northern B.C. coast with its crumbled totem poles, and Akutan was like another planet after the Gulf. Now we are moving along Davidson Bank past Sandman Reefs toward the Shumagin Islands, and once again we have entered a new perceptual movie, slid across the line into another dimension.

And another season. It was Indian summer, then autumn North Pacific, then a plunge into the miracle summer of Akutan. Now it is crystal early winter, breath fogging the glass, and the Penthouse is no longer the hearth. Even when we are awake we tend to stay in our sleeping bags in the Opium Den, wearing sweaters and sometimes scarves, or we gather in the galley to be near the big iron-topped stove, the only source of heat on the boat, which still bears its original name, M.S. AMBASSADOR, in faint rust-coloured letters. Hardly anybody stays out on deck – it is too damn cold. The four-hour watches seemed long when we came up the Inside Passage and stretched out into long stony trips on the Gulf. Now they are eternities of waiting.

We are starting to get tired. Conversations move more slowly and there are fewer babbling sessions. We are no less nervous – Cannikin looms large in our minds – but a kind of numbness is setting in. It's hard to keep your momentum up when you're moving away from your target. One afternoon Metcalfe and I were on watch, he sagging against the wheel, looking half-asleep like a dozing cat, as though melting away

The fishing vessel *Sleep Robber* pays a visit to the *Greenpeace*.

into another world. "The question is, Bob," he said, speaking from far away, "is this an Ahab trip or an Ishmael trip? Cannikin is Moby Dick, you know. For some of us, anyway. And you know, to this day I still don't know which one it is for me." He waited a while, and I waited a while, and then he seemed to return to the world of the lurching bobbing wagging waiting station, aware once again that he was holding the wheel. He looked at me evenly. "Do you? Know what it is, I mean? Are we madmen or orphans out doing a job? I remember that line of Melville's: 'There is death in this business of whaling.' Well, the whales are gone. Sometimes I feel like Ishmael looking at Ahab in horror. The Ahab part of me is mad enough to pull the lightning down from the sky. 'Leap! Leap up, lick the sky! I leap the burn with thee; I burn with thee!' He's obsessed and he scares me, because he doesn't give a shit about the *Pequod* or the *Greenpeace*. What was it Ishmael said about the *Pequod*? A noble old craft, but melancholy too. . . . Well, this old rig's a *Pequod* if there ever was one, and I can see it going down. 'And the great shroud of the sea' rolling on, and on, and on, 'oh, death-glorious ship! Oh lonely death on lonely life!' And then the other part of me who's in this century, not that one, says, Metcalfe old man, don't blow your cool, and I'm right back into the politics and press releases and news desk phone ringing at three in the morning and meetings in executive suites and plush carpets and the tinkle of martini glasses. Ishmael survived, but who remembers him? Ahab was the hero, and he was mad. Sometimes I think I'd rather be Ahab – I'd rather go down with the fucking whale."

"I'm not Ishmael, Ben," I said, "but neither are you. We're not Ahab either."

We have a strange intimacy, Metcalfe and I. We have jumped through the same hoops, inhabited the same small closed world of western Canadian journalism, worked at the same jobs – police beat, city hall, news desk, night city editor. But he did them almost thirty years before I did. By the time I arrived on the scene, scarcely any trace of him was left. Both of us dropped out of high school in Winnipeg, both of us went kicking and sweating through the same late-night pits of reporting and editing, and now our trajectories have come together on this noble but melancholy old boat. The bond is undeniable. Yet even at that moment, standing in the Penthouse, taking turns at the wheel, we both knew that a struggle was shaping up between us. We will face each other across the galley table and fight desperately, for our very lives and for control of the boat. Yet it will be more like a struggle with our own shadows than a direct fight. He can fight with Fineberg and Simmons easily enough, and even Bohlen, but not so easily with me, because I can't help but know the kind of punches he will throw. We have identical fight styles, but Metcalfe is thirty years older, thirty years tougher, with thirty years more training. He is strong. How strong? The only way to measure it is in the ring. When it comes down to the final battle for control of the *Greenpeace*, who will win?

But at this moment the struggle is not yet in focus. At this moment we are approaching Shumagin Island, just complying with the orders of the U.S. Coast Guard. We will head into Sand Point, Alaska, go through the red tape of formal entry through customs, which we should have done earlier, and then we will be faced with nothing more than a long wait for word on the test.

Funny about that bust. The Coast Guard had advised us we couldn't go into Dutch Harbor, but we could go into Akutan. They said nothing about having to make formal application for entry. It was enough to make you paranoid. *You can go in that room*, and then, *Aha! You're under arrest for trespassing!*

Sand Point

Into the Shumagin Islands we came sailing on this day, the day on which Cannikin was supposed to go off. We should be at Amchitka now, waiting for America's largest underground explosion to hit us, but instead we are almost 700 miles away, rounding the tip of an island called Unga, not Amchitka, up through Popof Strait to the cannery town of Sand Point, with the test still at least a month away.

Cormack angles the *Phyllis Cormack* in toward the dock, looking for a place to park among the dozens of fishing boats. Sand Point does not look like much, even though it is the largest community we have seen since Vancouver. How many light years away does Vancouver seem? The physical exhaustion of taking watches, of hauling oneself along against the walls and decks as they are flung about, and the months of excitement and tension and anticipation – all have taken their toll, and time seems to have lengthened. Can it be true that we have been on the boat a mere seventeen days? It feels like months. And yet we may still be in the early stage of the voyage. Another month before the bomb goes off, and then another two weeks before we make it back to Vancouver? A shiver goes through me. Sometimes the boat seems like a prison. Worse, I can feel my own determination crumbling, see the group's resolve fading on their faces.

Cormack jostles the boat in against the wharf. It's low tide – the pilings reach on up over our heads and we are staring between them into murky cold cavern-like glooms, the water milky and full of orange chips, and hundred of gulls yowk and crash up and down on the other side of the wharf to get at the bits of waste being discharged from the cannery. A wooden sign is nailed to one of the pilings beside the ladder leading to the top of the wharf. The bottom of the sign has been broken off, so all it says is PLEASE DO NOT. The air is cold and dank and there is a peculiar unpleasant smell. God, do we have to anchor right next to a stinking cannery? But we do – it seems there is nowhere else to put in.

Up on the wharf we are confronted by a long white warehouse with the name WAKEFIELD's printed on the side. And underneath, in smaller print, ALASKA KING CRAB. A forklift is trundling back and forth between six-foot-square wooden boxes and the entrance to the cannery. On each trip it carries a metal container over the edges of which we can see prickly crab legs and claws waving frantically. Then the container is flipped on its side with a pulpy eggshell-breaking sound, and a hundred or more Alaska king crabs go clicking and scratching down to a metal ramp, which carries them out of sight into the depths of the cannery. This is going to be a bummer.

Back at Akutan, Metcalfe and Keziere went aboard the sister ship of the *Pueblo*, the crab cannery boat, and Keziere came back as shaken and white-faced as when he was seasick. "Man," he said, "that's the worst place I've ever seen. No . . . reverence for life, or whatever you want to call it, *at all*. They just run those crabs through like old shoes, man, chop chop and tear them apart." Here at Sand Point it is the same. By the thousands the crabs are hauled up in nets, dumped into metal containers, forklifted over and piled in huge wooden bins, and then scooped up. Too bad if a leg gets sheared off or a claw or eye stalk gets torn out in the process.

Morbidly, we wander over to the wooden bins and look in. There is a constant rattle and *clickety-click-click*, like distant typewriter keys or paper clips, and we are peering into the pit. A dizzying swoop of emotion, like vertigo, and I am on the precipice of my childhood nightmares, which were filled with monsters just like these clacking mandible-wagging creatures. Backward and forward they plow, heaving desperately upward, only to slide back with a splash and be caught in a seething avalanche of prickly purplish armour, shells shuddering and convulsing, pincers groping wildly, long fragile feelers bent and broken and twisted. *Click click click.* For one gagging gasping moment I think I'm going to pass out. King crabs are possessed of some kind of consciousness, aren't they? They have families, they have tribes, they set up colonies as deep as seventy fathoms down, they migrate, they go hunting, they fight – some kind of consciousness, so how do they feel in that trap, especially the ones at the bottom? "Let the goddamn bomb go off, man," says Thurston. "The sooner this planet is rid of us, the better."

The whole story is that the crabs are caught in pots where they remain for as long as five days, starving, struggling desperately to get out. The boat comes along and they are hauled up, dumped in heaps into a water-filled hold, and carries them back to shore, which may take another day or two. Several more days may go by before the forklift hauls them up in nets, dripping and clacking, their snapped limbs dangling, and drops them into the bins. Within a day or two the crabs are swept down the chute into the cannery, where they are seized like coconuts and rammed against a fixed steel blade that looks like a battle axe. They are literally split in half. Their pincers tighten spasmodically at the moment of dying, with enough force to chop off a man's finger, so the workers keep their hands out of the way. Then, still twitching, the half bodies are tossed onto a conveyor belt and carried through a giant dishwasher-like apparatus. They are dismembered, canned, and shipped to the south, where people like us eat them as a delicacy.

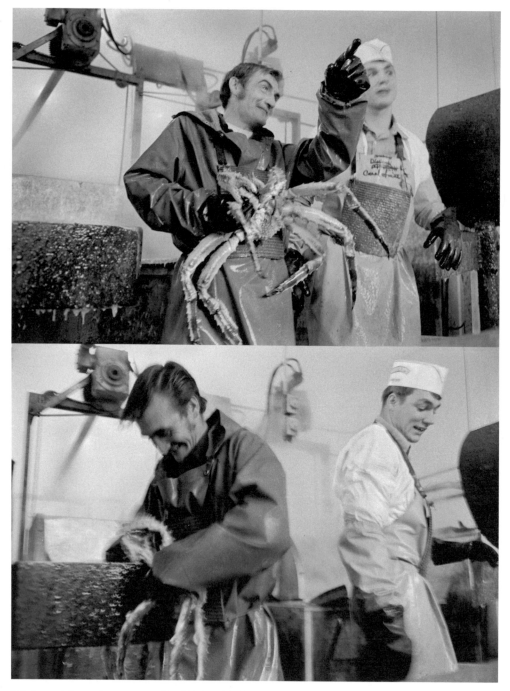

Workers at the crab cannery at Sand Point, Alaska.

Meanwhile, the cracked remains of the shells and the white mucus that spills out like broth are flushed into the water. The gulls dive down to feed and the stench hovers under the wharf like a cloud. It is in that very cloud, so different from the Surf-Cloud at Akutan, that the *Phyllis Cormack* is moored, while the forklift chugs and putts along the wharf, and the distant clicking of the trapped crabs tinkles in the air all day, all night. The record for an Alaska king crab is sixty-one inches across – wider than your kitchen table. But that was ten years ago. Since then, hordes of boats have gone out hunting for them. With the whales almost extinct, the herring at the edge of oblivion, the shrimp disappearing, and the halibut so scarce that boats have to push out into uncharted waters to find them, fishermen have turned increasingly to crabs. At first it was a bonanza, with regular hauls of creatures larger than German shepherds. But each year, as the plunder continues, they drop in size. And each year the "minimum allowable size" is lowered, just an inch at a time. Now, in the autumn of 1971, scarcely a decade after the great Alaska king crab industry became "commercially viable," it is on its last legs. The crabs piled in the bins at Sand Point average seven inches across the shell (twenty-four inches spread out), and fishermen and cannery workers are handling crabs with six- and even five-inch shells. We saw the abandoned canneries along the B.C. coast, we saw the abandoned whaling station at Akutan – just one of hundreds – and we do not have to be geniuses to see that the vast white Wakefield's Cannery will soon be as quiet as the one at Klemtu. Worse, the seas will be silent and lifeless, and there will be more human beings than ever, all starving to death in a stripped and looted world.

"There's two things we've gotta do before we leave here," I tell Thurston. "One is to get some black paint and scrawl all over the cannery wall: A CRAB IS YOUR BROTHER. And the other thing is to push those fucking bins over and free as many crabs as we can."

"Right on, Booby. You get the paint and I'll steal the forklift."

Sand Point is a bummer in other ways. Redneck-looking brutes shamble along the wharf, and at the general store, a guy wearing a cowboy hat, cowboy boots and mirror sunglasses comes out, looks our way, spits on the ground, then gets into his truck, starts the engine, and roars forward. For a second we are frozen in our tracks, not believing what's happening. But here comes the truck, across the planks toward us, and we can't see the bastard's eyes, hidden behind the mirror sunglasses. Almost too late, we catch on that he has no intention of slowing down, and six of us leap out of the way at the last second. The truck comes barrelling between us like a bowling ball skimming past the pins, and clatters and rumbles on up the hill. We're left there, shaking our fists and screaming obscenities. A dozen other redneck-looking characters lounge on the docks, staring stonily at us, no nods or greetings of any kind.

Later, back on the boat, Bohlen calls us together in the galley. "Look, we'd better recognize the fact that we're not in friendly territory. Most of these people don't know anything about us except that we're a bunch of political radicals, and this place reminds me of little towns in Texas. We'd better not make any assumptions about how welcome we are here. Especially you four with long hair. I think it would be wise if none of us went out alone. That bastard with the truck works for the local airline company, and that company has the contract to run supplies out to Amchitka for the AEC. I don't want us to all get paranoid, but then I wouldn't want anybody to get run over or beaten up or shot. "

The customs officer, a retired fisherman, comes down to the boat to tell us that the business of our customs violation is being dealt with by authorities in Anchorage, and that he will let us know as soon as possible what the decision is. In the meantime we will have to put up a $500 bond, and the nine Canadians on board may yet be fined $1,000 each for going ashore at Akutan. Bohlen makes an emergency phone call to Irving Stowe, one of the other executives of the Don't

Make a Wave Committee in Vancouver, to find out how much money we have left. Irving reports that he is expecting some donations from environmental and religious groups in the States, but the money hasn't come through yet. After paying the $500, we are running low on cash. So now, on top of everything else, we are going broke.

"Fuck it," Thurston says, when we are all feeling as low as we can go. "There must be a pub or something in this burg. I don't know about the rest of you, but I could use a drink."

"Wow, I dunno," Moore says. "The vibes are awful here."

"I wouldn't advise it," says Fineberg. "These little fishing towns can be pretty rough. Not as bad as they were a few years ago, but some story is always tucked away in the back pages of the Anchorage papers. Man Killed in Bar. Or Fisherman's Body Found Near Such-and-Such, Knife Sticking Out of His Back. This ain't the Summer of Love, my friends."

But first . . . there's a little red and grey metal telephone booth up on the wharf, past the cannery, right next to a laundromat and a musky garbage-littered building like a bus station that has free showers. At last! A telephone where we can communicate without having to scream every single word through the *eeeiiiiiiii sreeee yoooooooooo zit zit zit oiiiiiinnnnn ch cu cu zeeeeeeeeep* of the shipboard side-band radio. It is like entering the confessional, but in a mood of ecstasy, because it is finally possible to speak to someone without the whole crew overhearing. To step into this blessedly private telephone booth on the wharf, and to shut the door behind me! What relief, what a swift realization of just how badly I have missed uninhibited conversation. Metcalfe goes in first, alone with his wife at last, and the rest of us stand around outside the glass booth, talking animatedly with one another while gazing around at the cannery, the eclectic array of fishing boats, anywhere but at Metcalfe. We can't bear to watch half of a long-distance lovemaking session – it is too intense, what with our own shaky hunger to get through to our women.

And now up runs Darnell, puffing little clouds of steam as he comes. "Okay you guys," he says, leaping into our midst, "it's a fight to the death now! The last guy left standing gets to use the phone next." We all pull out imaginary machine guns and execute him, and he doubles up, riddled with bullets, and starts to crumble to the wharf. "Well," he says, "let's try." And we all start yelling, "Hurry up, Metcalfe! Just make it a quickie."

"Goddamn, he talks to Dorothy almost every night."

"Ah, come on. That wasn't very intimate."

In fact, our arrangement of Metcalfe as communications man and Dorothy as relay centre in their Vancouver living room is putting overwhelming pressure on Metcalfe. The few times the rest of us have managed to get through to our wives in the middle of the night have been exquisitely painful – the sound of her voice in your ear makes you ache to be with her. And tremendous backlogs of emotion are piling up in our heads, intensified by the knowledge that this may be the last time we'll ever talk to each other. Our wives are no less scared than we are at the idea of us sitting at the edge of a nuclear explosion, so each radio communication is another Goodbye-maybe-forever-I-love-you-I-wish-we-were-together-I-wish-this-wasn't-happening. The few times Keziere has got through to Lou, he is so shaken by his desire to be with her that he has gone out on deck and stood in the night rain and wind for twenty minutes, freezing to death, just to get a grip on himself again.

I am trembling by the time it is my turn on the Sand Point wharf telephone. I know exactly what I am in for – I have seen the others stumble out, pain on their faces. *God, I want to be with her!* Yeah, the trip has taken more out of us than we admit. We are frightened, nowhere near as casual about the whole business as we pretend, if only to stop ourselves from crying like little boys. Life is so sweet! Why take these chances with it? We'll all be wiped out in the end anyway. Why not be with the human beings that you love and "get it while you can," as Janis Joplin sang?

Zoe's voice, Zoe's beautiful gutsy strong musical magnificent voice slashes into my ear like a razor, as though she is in the next room. I'm gulping for words, "Zoe, I . . . I . . . I. . . ." Tears leap across my eyes. It was idiotic to have Metcalfe and Dorothy serve as the communications officers. It was like putting the astronaut's wife in the space centre and telling her to give her husband the order to disengage his module from the lunar orbiter and take the plunge into the fifty-fifty chance of death. All along we have been so envious of Metcalfe because he gets to talk to his wife so much. Now we know that it has been agony for both of them. *So close. So far. I want you.* My kids come on the line, jabbering madly and urgently, trying to tell me absolutely everything that's happened to them. "So and so took my tricycle and Zoe went over and got it back and the cat's gonna have kittens any day Zoe says and the teacher gave me a blue star for a drawing I did of a duck sorta like the ducks in that book that Nanny gave us for Christmas you know that one we changed all the colours with paints and you know what? Tomorrow we're going over to. . . ."

Emotional overload. I reel out of the booth and go over and lean against the laundromat wall, gasping for breath. *What am I doing here? Fuck around, let's go home! We're just kidding ourselves – we can't do anything anyway. The whole Earth doom is coming down too fast, man. We're half-poisoned already. Why bother?*

Well, that's cool for *you* to cop out, but what kind of looks are your kids going to give you ten or twenty or thirty years from now when the whole shebang comes crashing down and they die of leukemia or cancer or bone-rot or DDT, or they are driven mad by overcrowding, or wiped out in a nuclear war, and they ask us, Why did you let this happen? The environmental destruction of the world is going on everywhere, in plain view, so anyone who carries on business as usual, or sits on their ass

Metcalfe calls home on a land line for the first time since leaving Vancouver.

or keeps their head buried in the sand, is an accomplice in the crime of murdering the future. We are all of one mind in this belief, our wives and lovers no less than ourselves, and though we all falter and grow weak and lose faith in our vision of a reverently tended green planet where our children and grandchildren and great-grandchildren might live a blessed life, the vision surges up again and again, sometimes in waves of overwhelming power, other times just in quivers. "We love you, Greenpeace, Oh yes we do. . . ."

But now, after ecstasies and agonies of phone calls home comes the sheer joy of getting into the showers – cold and dirty as they are – and grabbing a bar of soap and washing away all the sweat and sea stink and boat smells. From the showers we go to the laundromat – clean clothes! – and from the laundromat down to the liquor store to buy some wine, beer, and rum. The Don't Make a Wave Committee may be going broke, but Fineberg has an Alaska chequing account and we all borrow money from him wildly, writing Canadian cheques, becoming giddy at the thought of such luxuries as clean bodies and clean clothes and sleeping bags and ice-cold beer. Wow! Maybe Sand Point won't be so bad after all.

That night, despite Fineberg's warning, Thurston, Keziere, Cummings, Darnell, Moore and I head down to the local bar, the Sand Point Tavern. It looks heavy enough – short-haired suspicious-eyed super hard-rock characters, a couple of actual peroxide blondes, guys with cowboy hats and buckskin jackets, lumberjack-shirted scar-faced Aleuts, beefy meathook-handed whites, and a couple of guys wearing flight jackets, probably from the airline company with the contract to take stuff out to Amchitka. The waiter is a dark-haired mean-looking son of a bitch with a scar that winds like a trench across his whole face, from his hairline, over his broken nose, to the right side of his chin, where it ends in a cleft as though a wedge of bone has been taken out. A jukebox blares raunchy western music, but nobody dances, and at exactly the moment in which the six of us come tromping in through the swinging door in our Greenhawk uniforms, the music whangs to an end, leaving only the electronic buzz of the jukebox hanging in the air. Nothing fills the silence but the squeak of chairs and the odd clink of a glass as every single one of the super-heavies in that place turns and looks at us. Shit, we are gonna get killed. But nothing to do except keep on coming in, trying to look cool and vaguely tough ourselves. Darnell and Cummings look like they might be able to acquit themselves pretty well in a fight, but Thurston, Keziere, Moore, and I won't stand a chance. Hey, what am I saying? I'm the guy with his Purple Belt in karate – and Jesus, maybe those guys are counting on me to do something if we get jumped!

But it's all a weird hallucination. A moment later, the heavy-looking dudes have all gone back to their drinks, rapping away, the glasses clinking. Another western song is coming to life from the fluorescent whale teeth of the jukebox, the waiter is running about yakking and joking and being a good-time Charlie, and this is just a regular bar. If any of them actually had looked at us when we came in, which is not at all certain, it was out of curiosity. That's what paranoia does – it causes hallucinations. And that's why paranoid guys like the ones who are building the bomb at Amchitka can't be trusted. They're hallucinating and they don't even know it. It's a chilling thought. The doomsday machine is not a fantasy any longer. It is the Nuclear Deterrent System, liable to go off accidentally at any second, and the guys with their fingers twitching weirdly on the buttons are tripping through some paranoid hallucinogenic universe, and *they think they're sane.* As Bohlen says, "Living in this world, if you're not paranoid, you're crazy."

We stay five hours at the Sand Point Tavern. We get to know a lot of the guys, we ignore others, and they ignore us. We yuk it up with the scar-faced waiter and blow about five bucks in the jukebox. Thurston gets up and asks a fifty-year-old woman to dance, then I get dancing with her and then a couple of other older women. We work our way down to the younger ones but stay away from the ones with boyfriends. We order round after round of drinks, somebody at another table orders a round for us, and several fishermen crowd in around our table rapping about that goddamn bomb and "Sure hope you fellas can do something about it, no damn good for the fishing, and fishing's getting hard enough as it is." They tell us that the halibut catch per man per boat this year is down fourteen percent from this time last year, and there are signs that the shrimp are starting to avoid the banks even south of Sanak, where they've always run heavy this time of year, and furthermore blah blah blah. We are rapping away, swearing, laughing, playing the raunchiest music on the jukebox, and Thurston is dancing like a crazy zonked-out lumberjack. Younger guys detach themselves from their tables and wander over to tell us how bad that storm was they had back in April and what you've got to watch out for once you get up around the Rat Islands – not so much the rip tides, though they're bad too if you don't bide your time so as to ride with them through the straits, but them kelp beds. Yep, kelp beds like nowhere else in the world. Whaddya think all them otters are up there for, the weather? Har har har har. As long as our boat's fine, we're fine, they tell us, unless we try to stay out in the open where we aren't welcome.

At 3 a.m. we stumble back past the house trailers and prefab houses, corrugated sheet metal Quonset huts – hey, at least there's one yard full of real spruce trees here, and they're all blowing and flapping in the wind, Christ it's cold, hiccup, stumble, fall, laugh, clatter across the wharf yelling at the floodlit cannery, "A brother's yer crab!" Or – what is it? – "A crab's yer mom! Yer mom's a crab!" Oooops, pick me up. Hey, fuck around, *help!* When we come skidding and banging and half-crashing down onto the deck of the boat, Cormack is sitting in the galley, lights on, with Bohlen and Birmingham, Cormack with his big hands wrapped around a china mug, Birmingham reading a western,

Thurston.

Bohlen in his long underwear, hair a mess, building a tiny geodesic dome with broken toothpicks and cut-up bits of paper – and they look like three pissed-off fathers.

"Where the hell you dummies been?" Cormack says. "Thought you might'a been lynched by now, though it'd serve you bloody well right, goddamn loonies."

"I was just going to hit the sack," says Bohlen, not wanting to admit to any paternal feelings toward us zonked-out drunken bums.

Birmingham wants to know all about the bar. "Hot dang! Never been in one of those places, you understand. All them hot-to-trot gals and all that. Go-go girls and all." Everybody laughs, because we know by now that Birmingham is a genius – he has almost finished single-handedly building a whole submarine in his back yard, and whenever he gets mad enough to make an observation, he's always right on. Yet he's got this old geezer act down pat, the stereotypical by-crickety dang-it-all guy. Still, it's a good act, and he seems content in it, and let's face it, it's pretty safe, so we don't hassle him. End of Saturday Night in Sand Point.

SUNDAY, OCTOBER 3, 1971

Whoops! In the morning there are a few hangovers and generally a numbed mood about the boat. We peck a bit at our typewriters, trying to dream up columns to send off to the papers. As usual Metcalfe works in longhand on his Monday morning CBC commentary. Other guys write letters home, Bohlen finishes off his toothpick-and-paper dome, the customs officer drops by to chat, several fishermen come down and lay some gifts of halibut and crab on us, we sip a few beers, Darnell cooks up an incredible supper, the galley windows get steamed up, it gets dark outside, boat engines start up, *slap slap slap* of little waves. The cannery has been closed all day, gulls trailing desolately over the buildings. No crab slaughter today, but the restless hopeless *click click click* still comes across the wharf from the bins. A thin rain puddles the beams. The wind is chill. And still no word about when the bomb will go off.

TUESDAY, OCTOBER 5, 1971

When we arrived, the wharf around the cannery was surrounded by boats, with only a few parking spaces left. But now, boats and more boats are double-parked and in some places triple-parked. The fishing fleets are retreating from the October gales coming up out on the Shumagin Bank, and points beyond. The autumn equinox is stirring the seas into a furry. "Yeah, it was startin' to smoke out there," the fishermen say, referring to a wind so hard it sends spray out from the waves and spreads it across the surface of the water like soupy mist. When it starts to smoke, the fishermen leave their nets and pots and run like hell.

Besides fishing boats, there are converted navy supply ships, now used for running gear up to oil companies and mining depots; smart new steel-hulled trawlers, which look more like pleasure craft with leatherette foam-padded swivel seats up at the wheel; old moss-and-slime-covered one-man wooden rigs, like outhouses with tiny windows mounted on rowboats; and proud old gumwood-hide packers, the real vets. No two boats are the same. Some look like houseboats, some scarcely as wide across as a man with his legs and arms stretched out, others even longer than the eighty-foot *Phyllis Cormack,* and some as bulky and graceless as the crates that hold heavy machinery. Some look like the Little Red Caboose, or PT boats, or castles mounted on Noah's ark. Some are covered with so much grease and slime from decades of fish scales being crushed under gumboots that it looks as though their decks were coated with grey nail polish. Others are painted with bright green enamel, or their wood is nothing more than peeling piss-coloured varnish. There are old sheds, shoeboxes, freight cars, sports cars – an unending variety of sizes and ages and types of boats. Masts and rigging swing back and forth like sagging cobwebs and the rifles of hundreds of hunters all try to get a bead on the same flock of passing ducks, each taking aim at a different bird, each adjusting and readjusting his aim. The water is choppy and there is a constant squeak of rubber tires and buoys rubbing against wood, the *skreek skreek* of hulls against the barnacles on the pilings, the *flop flap whack* of thick wet ropes strung from boats to wharf, and the howl of the wind as it drives the clouds furiously against the distant blue peaks of the peninsula and the islands all around. Whitecaps are clearly to be seen even out in the sheltered waters of Popof Strait, and out in the open, the waves are reported to be rising to heights of sixty and seventy feet.

Down at the tavern, the men just in off the boats tell incredible stories of taking green water over the stern just as they rounded Mountain Point at the tip of Nagai Island. Winds that have been a whispering among the gulls and terns and puffins in the morning have changed into leagues of dark grey smoking water by early afternoon. Guys tell us about the waters farther up the chain, how as you approached the end, around Amchitka, you took blasts of wind that had been building right across the Bering Sea. Three guys got caught up by the Pribilof Islands, a few hundred miles north of the Aleutians, out in the unbelievably vast and lonely sweeps of the Bering, and had to hang on for fourteen days in a 180-mile-an-hour bitch of a storm. Only thing you can do then is get that anchor down as far as she'll go, face her into the waves, gear right down, and jog for your life. Waves come in at 120 feet. Usually you keep losing ground – the anchor can't hold against that kind of competition – but the trick is to handle her like a kite, with a baby-pin hanging on to

Darnell.

the ground and you up in the kite, in the middle of the goddamnedest hurricane you ever saw, and you gotta keep steering so's you're aimed right into that wind and hope the baby-pin don't come loose completely from whatever little bitty patch of gravel she's grappling at, 'cause without that anchor, you ain't got a chance. Boat just flips around, the 120-footers come down over the roof, and that's at least a couple of hundred tons of water hitting you like a paddle. A lot of boats break up. Others just kind of lie down and die. Still others flip right over. Yeah, she's rough.

Everybody we talk to in Sand Point has at least one relative who drowned out there, and everybody can name at least a dozen guys they knew who have gone down. It is like a perpetual state of war – every time Daddy goes out, well, he may not come back, and that's the way it is. "Holy smoke," says Moore, visibly shaken by all these yarns. "I didn't know it would be like this."

We are all shaken. Cummings is getting a desperate look, Keziere is growing numb, we start losing interest in heading down to the tavern. An afternoon in that place, listening to the fishermen, an awful lot of them with a missing finger or hand or eye, or a moon-pit face from when a big one came over the side and shattered a window and sent shrapnel into whoever was sitting in the galley, the wind keening around the rafters, the glass panes clattering even here in the lee of the island, icy blasts hitting us like blows as we come clambering out of the bar – it is the stuff of nightmares. In my dreams I lie at the bottom of the sea as vengeful Alaska king crabs hop across the seabed like colossal purple tarantulas, their pincers reaching out, a small black lightbulb eye looking squarely into my own, and I convulse helplessly, lungs like waterbeds, trying to speak, trying to shout, *"Crab, I'm your brother!"*

Then there is the story about Old Jock, the Alley-oot who was on the *Annabelle* when she went down outside of Port Miller. The rest of the guys were running around drunk as skunks, trying to get the lifeboat loose, but Old Jock had put in forty-five years in these waters and he knew what to do. He put on about three pairs of thermal underwear, all the socks he could find, T-shirts, sweaters, jackets, overcoats, three pairs of mitts, and wrapped his whole head in towels, slung a bunch of life jackets around his legs and arms, and stayed there in the bunkhouse until she started to break up. Never found a trace of the rest of the guys, not a sign of the lifeboat, but Old Jock – well, they found him three days later. Alive, all right. Now, that water's *cold*. If you go down in that water without a wetsuit, you're a dead man in – well, usually takes a minute or two. Of course fishermen can't be going around in wetsuits all day – never get any work done. So Old Jock was alive, but the sand fleas had got at him. By the time he was pulled up on deck, and they got around to cutting off all the soaked coats and jackets – no one able to believe he had stayed alive in those waters three whole days and two nights, but then he was a tough old bastard, never came any tougher – and peeling off the last few layers of underwear and T-shirts, they could tell it was no use. You could feel the bugs wiggling and bumping around, all over him and multiplying by the handful. Yeah, sand fleas do that – get inside your clothes, sometimes even a wetsuit. Usually they go for the armpits and the little spaces behind your balls first, and start chomping away. When they fished out Old Jock, the bugs had got at his whole belly, even worked their way in from under the armpits, almost to his lungs. His balls were gone for sure, and the toes – he was pretty much down to bone and a bit of meat. Everything except his head, because he'd wrapped it up so tightly in towels.

By this point in the story, we are all trembling. No one dares to ask the question: could he still think?

Somebody gets the idea of sending for a dozen wetsuits and we have a terrific argument about it. I own a wetsuit and did not bring it along, because it seemed absurd – like taking a life jacket with you on a jumbo jet flying over the ocean ten miles up. If that baby goes down, no life jacket's going to save you. I argue fiercely against the wetsuit plan. Tempers flare, and in the end there is a consensus to get the wetsuits – "consensus" meaning that only a couple of us are in disagreement and the issue isn't worth the energy it would take to fight about it. We spend a surrealistic evening in the galley while Thurston measures us all and calls out the numbers. Ankle to knee, seventeen inches; knee to crotch, twelve; elbow to wrist, ten; elbow to shoulder, eleven. Bohlen writes down all the figures and places dozens of calls to Vancouver, reading the figures out, while people back home run around trying to get hold of the wetsuits. All because we are getting unnerved by the horror stories we are picking up at the bar. We are afraid that maybe this is going to be a lot lot *lot* worse than we thought. It is one thing to go to the gates of hell, and another to drown along the way. And then there were the sand fleas, and. . . .

Each day, reports arrive, either from the Don't Make a Wave Committee or Dorothy Metcalfe, or through conversations with people at home, or through my calls to *The Vancouver Sun*, or Fineberg and Simmons' calls to Pittsburgh, San Francisco, Chicago, and points between, still clawing around for that tiny data-point: *when?* It is good to know that environmentalists in Washington, D.C., the very coalition of high-powered legal beagles who successfully halted the Supersonic Transport program – no minor feat that – are hacking and chopping at the Amchitka program with the same energy they have brought to bear on the supersonic transport aircraft. Some days, small victories are scored. Other days, potentially large victories are scored. We also have setbacks, and days when the battle lines seem frozen, neither side gaining or losing an inch. Like cavemen armed with ballpoint spears, the band of environmentalists are gradually forcing the mastodon into a corner. It is bleeding a bit and limping, but not seriously hurt, and at any moment it may turn with a roar and come charging through their ranks, scattering them like leaves.

It's October.

WEDNESDAY, OCTOBER 6, 1971

Word comes through that a demonstration in front of the U.S. Consulate's office in Vancouver attracted 10,000 students! School boards and principals had refused to allow time off from school to attend the demonstration, yet from all over Vancouver and surrounding areas, from as far away as the town of Hope, ninety miles east, the kids came. It was a Children's Crusade – they skipped classes in droves and converged on downtown Vancouver, filling up the street in front of the Consulate's office and spilling over into nearby streets and sidewalks and parking lots. It was the largest demonstration in Vancouver's history. On the boat, we hang around the radio room all afternoon, jammed together around Metcalfe, hanging on to every word being reported by Dorothy. All our wives and girlfriends and kids are downtown with the kids. Several of us break down and weep. I find myself out on the bow, crying as I have not cried for years – with joy, as people cried during the world wars when news came of a major victory. *Ten thousand kids!*

The old feeling is back, but it has metamorphosed into a different kind of awe, having nothing to do with miraculous coincidences or planet love. This is pure, sweet, flawlessly human awe, a feeling of unaloneness, of being borne along on a great current of history, of being in touch with your people and time and society. The effect of the demonstration is to fire us as we have not been fired before. "How far?" somebody yells, and in a chorus, we scream, *"All the way!"* We even borrowed the lines from a John Wayne movie. What a satisfying synch *that* was! A couple of days after our arrival in Sand Point, the local movie house, a metal Quonset hut, showed *The Green Berets*, and naturally we went down to see it. Into the theatre trooped the Greenhawks to confront the image of the Green Berets. It is possibly the worst film I've ever seen. Thurston and I gave up after twenty minutes and stalked out and went down to the bar. "So that's what they're like," Thurston mutters, meaning the whole bundle of assholes from John Wayne to the Atomic Energy Commission, with Dick Nixon and the U.S. Army included. They *are* madmen! But there were a few good lines in the movie. At one point, one of the "heroes" in the movie says, as they rise in a helicopter to go murder some more Vietnamese, "This trip'll make LSD look like an aspirin." The Greenhawks screamed with laughter, although no one in the theatre laughed with us. Yep, our own trip is making LSD look like an aspirin. "How far?" yells John Wayne to a passing phalanx of shaven androids, and, *click,* C-90 psychotronic tape having been slotted into place, they respond: *"All the way!"*

"You know the worst part of it all," said Thurston, slumped at our table in the bar, "John Wayne's probably real. What does that do to your sense of cosmic justice, Booby? Shoots it all to fucking hell, doesn't it? Grand pianos, man. Grand pianos. *The Green Berets.* Barf, upchuck, puke, and all that. Oh Christ, blow the bomb! Let's get it over with. Let the ants take over, man. Or even the sand fleas. I don't give a shit any more."

Old Jock wrapped in all those layers of clothes, bobbing helplessly in the icy kill-a-man-in-one-minute waves, being hurled seventy feet in the air, riding like a cork, absolutely unable to move because he's got so much clothing on, the towels blinding him, whirled through those fierce rollercoaster plunges, wind coming at him a hundred miles an hour – can he hear the shrieking speed-crazed sea witch taking the final leap into the mind catacombs of total freakout? He knows the sand fleas will come, but he can't move his arms or legs to claw the life jackets free and sink blissfully into numbness. Now, after eternities inside eternities of waiting to be transported into death, the life spark dulled enough that he does not feel the seething sand flea colonies first mining the pores in his skin and then, in nibbling tearing masses of thousands, stripping away his flesh and organs. No longer can he even twitch, let alone unbuckle the life jackets. He is doomed to a very long dying, and that's what you get for fighting so hard to live, Old Jock!

Oh yes, you're the jaw muscles writhing within the wads of towel to keep opening the mouth for another breath of air, and not knowing whether it's going to be air or water that finally penetrates the masks that smother and strangle you. You don't know which way is up.

Oh, the dreams are getting bad at night. I wake up in the small dark space of the Opium Den, sweat gone putrid hanging in the air, and guys in the galley arguing or babbling away, each guy so familiar by now that I already know what he's going to say on any given subject. It is maddening to have to pretend to listen – or worse, to say anything myself, because my own act, my own set of pre-programmed responses, my own bullshit, are just as transparent and obvious, and communication has become a treadmill – *Christ, I can't stand it.* I awake from the dream of being Old Jock, back in my little coffin-sized bunk, the jerk-off curtain closed, pitch black darkness all around except for a silhouette visible through the porthole – spooky-looking wharf pilings covered with barnacles. All too familiar voices echo from the galley, Cummings, Moore, and Bohlen doing their routines, the same old blather, the same old bullshit, the same goddamn con games and psychological manouevrings, each guy locked into the trap of being himself, no other. And so no real growth takes place, no evolution, no breakthroughs into new lands of understanding. We are trapped in moulds like toy soldiers. None of us, not even the freest wildest craziest soul on board – and surely we are an usually free wild crazy bunch to begin with – can break free and become something beyond himself, something better.

Lying in my bunk, struggling against panic as Old Jock must have struggled, I can feel my mind whirling through the sea witch's freakout scream – and yeah, I am starting to crack up. The notes in my log book go like this: Sept. 22, Weds. So this is what numbness is all about . . . Sept. 27, Mon. So this is what they mean by heaven . . . Sept. 30, Thurs. So this is frustration . . . Oct. 3, Sun. So now I know what they mean by terror . . . Oct. 5, Tues. Here's real homesickness. And now, desperately

Metcalfe and Thurston.

pulling the chain on my naked little light bulb, *not the dark any longer!* I reach for the log book, shaking, gulping a bit as I write: This is either claustrophobia or insanity. Schizophrenia? Panic? Emotional exhaustion? No, I think I'm just going crazy.

On the other guy's faces I see the same wild look that I saw on my own face when I dared to look in the mirror. Lines all over my forehead like a road map and fantastic hollows developing under my cheekbones. The look is subtle, the chin has vanished into a gritty stubble of hair, but a skull-face is emerging, so now I half-close my eyes each time I walk past the mirror. And the other guys are beginning to get that same look. Cummings has a permanent mad light in his eyes. Moore stares out into Old Jock nightmare land. Thurston grows crankier and bitchier and less tolerant of everybody. He shouts at Cormack, at Cummings, at Birmingham. But they are all shouting too. Cormack always shouts – we hardly ever hear him just talk – and he has been like this since the beginning. Maybe *we* are getting like *him*. Times when I think I'm just casually rapping away, I suddenly realize from the faces of the other guys that I've been shouting again. Oops! Slow down. Wind 'er down there, baby. Coooool 'er out.

Some guys are less flappable than others. Metcalfe still speaks in that soft controlled purring voice – the voice of an aristocrat – but now there are breakdowns even in that humming machinery. Now, more and more frequently, a harsh tense uncool tone sneaks through, and Metcalfe's image in my mind grows a bit fuzzy, then blurred, and then it begins to come apart at the seams and suddenly there is a complete stranger sitting across the table from me, an enemy, a man somehow threatening me. Where has Uncle Ben gone? Where is the guy who kept us in fits of laughter all across the Gulf, who dragged out those ancient Broadway musical tunes?

We have all got into the habit of singing "Would You Like to Swing on a Star?" But we replace the last word in the main lyric with our own weird combinations. "Or would you rather be a horny old man?" "Or would you rather be a chocolate-bar-crazed sea captain?" "Or would you rather be a . . . *sand flea-eaten corpse?*" Old father image mature war veteran cool hip all together Uncle Ben has gone through some awful transformation. So has everybody else. The social games we played with each other at first have given way. We have begun to slide in and out of our very own self-images, and the images we project on each other have begun to shift. What is going on? Are they really changing, or is my perception getting distorted? Has Moore, the guy I understood to be one of the iron radicals, really changed into a more gentle lovable sensitive character, almost a flower child, or is the pressure getting to me? Maybe I was wildly off the mark when I formed my first impression of him, way way way back (it seems like years ago) when we first got together on the boat. Cormack seemed like such a big tough no-talking bulldozer of a man, and now he reminds me of a beloved old uncle of mine who was always babbling and yakking and rapping away, couldn't shut him up. Who has changed, Cormack or me? I saw Cummings as strong and rock solid, but now he's strung out so tight that he'll crack like an egg if I so much as knock at his head with my knuckle. Or am I projecting my own tension and anxiety on him? What about Birmingham, docile and absurdly subservient, going hard as nails, getting angry more and more often, turning into an argumentative speed-rapping guy? And where has Bohlen gone? In his place a drawn-looking old man, half-slumped over the table, with the occasional flash of the old elf-humour or a twinkle in the eye. On and on it goes.

MONDAY, OCTOBER 11, 1971

The trouble is, the voyage did not just get underway – how long ago? God, almost a month! No, it got underway two years ago, just before the 1969 test at Amchitka. Six thousand university students rushed down to the U.S.–Canada border south of Vancouver and sealed it for the first time since the War of 1812. Some 10,000 Canadians across the country did the same in protest against testing at Amchitka. In the days that followed, several newly formed environmental groups, including the Sierra Club and the Don't Make a Wave Committee, got together to dream up an even more effective demonstration against the next test. Bohlen worked with both groups from the beginning, Moore was in on it, Darnell coined the word "Greenpeace" to name the various alliances under one umbrella, and Bohlen's wife Marie came up with the idea of sending out a boat to establish a floating picket line. One by one over the next two years, the rest of us joined in, as volunteers. Fineberg was the only one who didn't get involved until shortly before the boat departed. Captain John Cormack knew what he was in for a year ahead of time, when he agreed to charter his boat for the trip, and Birmingham joined up several months ago, when Cormack phoned him up and asked him. So we pushed and strained for a long time to get the trip underway, and we have lived under the shadow of Cannikin for at least a year on average, and we have put in thousands of man-hours of organizing, planning, political wrangling, and the rest. In a way we were exhausted even before we set foot on the boat. Now, with everything going wrong that can possibly go wrong – the test being delayed further every day, a ruling overturned in a lower court, a new suit launched from one place, another from somewhere else, more and more politicians speaking out against the test, demonstrations building in pitch, pressure mounting steadily – the worst part of it is that we can't just get our confrontation over with. We can only hang on and try to hold our position until the issue is resolved one way or another. Then we will either have our face-to-face encounter with Cannikin or we will not, and for the first time in history, an H-bomb test will have been cancelled. It is all so goddamn important, and yet here I am in my bunk, gasping for air, being driven to the edge by such petty matters as Cummings' habit of using my typewriter, Fineberg's butt-picky way of quibbling endlessly about minor strategic points, the sound of Thurston's laughter which stings me like an electric shock, and Cormack's inability to talk rather than yelling all the time. And everybody's getting just like him, shouting about nothing.

No, no, *stop*. Got to get a perspective on this thing. All this trivial bickering – surely to God we're above that. Ten thousand kids. Presidential candidates and B.C. Natives and Coast Guard guys expressing support. Border blockades, the Prime Minister, tens of thousands of people signing petitions and marching in the streets. Zoe has started an all-night vigil in front of the U.S. Consulate's office in Vancouver, out there with our kids and the other guys' wives and lovers, and they will stay there until the *Greenpeace* comes home – if it comes home. It *must* be real! It *must* matter! But each day we proceed farther down into the valley. Each day our arguments are powered less by reason and more by emotion. We try to cling to the reason – the reason we are out here, the reason to keep struggling, the reason for being. "Reason is a season," says Thurston. "Then there's a new season, and reason means something else. One man's magic is another man's routine. One man's truth is another man's lie. Philosophy is so fucking easy, man. It's cheap as shit." Pages torn from notebooks and scribbled with aphorisms are starting to appear on the walls of the galley.

MASTURBATION IS THE PREROGATIVE OF THE
   ESTABLISHMENT PRESS
IN VIOLENCE IS THE PRESERVATION OF SOCIAL ORDER
FROM TERROR ONE ESCAPES SCREAMING
BUT FEAR HAS A STRANGE SEDUCTION
REALITY: A FEDERAL OR PROVINCIAL RESPONSIBILITY?
TODAY IS EITHER THE FIRST AND/OR LAST DAY OF THE REST
   OF YOUR LIFE

TAKE THE "EGO" OUT OF ECOLOGY

NO! PUT IT BACK IN!

DEEP INSIDE EVERY NEWSPAPERMAN THERE IS A WHORE

    STRUGGLING TO BE LET OUT

A CRAB IS YOUR CAPTAIN

A FLOWER IS YOUR MIND

A SAND FLEA IS YOUR BROTHER

GOD IS ZENO'S PARADOX

ZENO'S PARADOX IS YOUR BROTHER

THIS TRIP'LL MAKE ZENO'S PARADOX LOOK LIKE AN

    ASPIRIN

Zeno's Paradox goes like this: Take the distance between two points and cut it in half. Then take the distance between the two new points and cut that in half. Take those two points and cut that distance in half. According to Zeno, if you have instruments precise enough to do it, you can keep on halving the distance and never at any moment will the two points come together. That is exactly the feeling we have – the two points are Vancouver and Amchitka, and we will never get there.

The arguments around the galley table are getting jagged at the edges, like broken beer bottles. Old hassles, such as whether Dick Fineberg was a CIA agent, seem long ago, far away, and downright quaint. Such a trifling issue, and safe in a clearly defined frame – objective: Amchitka. There was a game-like quality to the bickering in those days. Somewhere in the back of my mind I was constantly, frantically taking notes – got to remember that line! Uh oh, look what's going on over here! And laughing at the whole show, which was a gas. Grand pianos, man – how did you ever get yourself into this scene?

But all that has changed. All of us are being flushed out into the open. The cracks that we make about each other are like razors now. Before, when we were all united in our objective – getting to Amchitka –

we pulled our punches. Our meetings on the way up the Inside Passage had the quality of boys gathering in the pub after a day's work. Out on the Gulf of Alaska, the meetings were less chummy, more formal. They became forums, but there were rules, and the mood was almost pure board room. By Akutan, our meetings were veering in the direction of encounter sessions, with the board-room lid holding, but shaky.

The Sand Point meetings are something else. They have the stamp of psychodrama. The objective has gone out of focus. Initially it was Amchitka or bust, but now we have been busted, so what is the point of the exercise? Do we want simply to sail up to Amchitka as tourists, coincidentally arriving on the day of Cannikin's awakening? Was Amchitka our goal, or Cannikin? The two used to mean exactly the same thing, but now, although Amchitka is still within reach – we can start out tomorrow and head straight for the place – Cannikin has taken wing from its nest. It is no longer a specific time or place. It has started to leap nimbly about – it seems to want to play tag.

Money was a problem. Thurston is losing about a hundred bucks a day maintaining his practice while he is away, Moore, Keziere, and Bohlen all stand to lose their jobs if they are not back within six weeks, Metcalfe's freelance work is going all to hell, and Birmingham is feeling the pinch. And a new division has opened within the ranks. Some of us are getting paid for this work and some aren't. Fineberg turned down his grant to be part of the crew, but that has freed him from deadlines and work schedules. Moore gave up his teaching job at Simon Fraser University, so he has no deadline either. Cummings is on assignment for *The Georgia Straight* and can stay out here as long as the story lasts. Darnell is still getting his pittance as a volunteer for the Company of Young Canadians, and I am still getting paid for writing my column for *The Vancouver Sun*. What has all that to do with the good fight, the battle to stop the bomb, the crusade to head off environmental ruin? There were different sets of needs, different demands, different personal situations. In an army, everybody is more or less in the same boat, but on the *Greenpeace,* we are not in the same boat. Resentment against me, the paid *Sun* writer, for instance, was kept nicely under control. Nobody was in it for the money, and my column was helping the cause, so it could be forgiven.

At the outset, the fact that the protest was middle class seemed to have its advantages. We have jobs and families, so we cannot be dismissed as crackpots. But now our middle-class status is starting to take its toll. For us it was not "you have nothing to lose but your chains," but: "you have lots to lose." Still, other questions are more critical. Has our purpose been to focus public attention on the insanity of nuclear testing, with special reference to the extravagant hazards at Amchitka? Or has our purpose been to put our bodies across the tracks of the oncoming nuclear troop train? Which is it, a picket line protest, or a life-or-death fight to the finish? A trap door has opened neatly beneath us, and we have to define our goals more precisely, adjust to the new situation, reappraise all our goals, re-examine all our assumptions. Split hairs, nit-pick, cross-examine, review, re-evaluate, re-examine, regurgitate. Are we revolutionaries or reformers? If you look at anything too closely it becomes something else. Magnify a smooth surface just five times and it becomes a scabby shoal. Magnify it ten times and it's a ruin of craters and pots and wounds. Magnify it a hundred times and the surface becomes another universe completely. A thousand times and it's another dimension.

Desperately we try to keep the smooth surface in focus, but it is useless. We are faced with a different situation. Should we approach it in the same way we approached the original situation? Or do we have to change our line of attack? We have managed to bring the full weight of Canada to bear against the test, and what more can we do? Except for the brief flurry of press about the near-mutiny of the *Confidence* crew, the American media have ignored us, so there is not much we

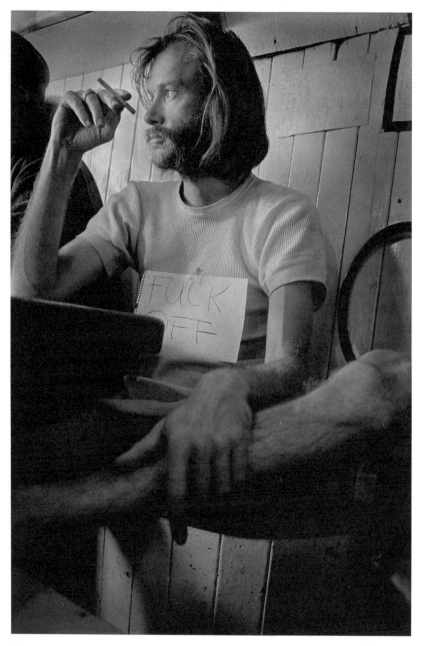

Hunter.

can do to apply the kind of pressure in the U.S. that we have in Canada – short of being gored by Cannikin. But was our goal to cause political embarrassment? Or was it to raise awareness of the dangers of nuclear testing, which awareness will grow enough to transform the political apparatus itself? On and on and on. We have begun to split apart under the weight of such questions.

Perhaps the divisions are inevitable. As Metcalfe noted back on the Gulf, we are a "disparate group," with different backgrounds and different minds and vastly different ways of looking and seeing and understanding things. With a great psychic *rrrrrrriiiiiiiiiiiiiiiiiiiip*, the *Greenpeace* is torn in half. The hope of achieving "consensus" is no longer even a hallucination – it has become a fairy tale. I cannot quite pinpoint the moment it happened, and I do not know whether it has been happening all along, but the moment came when we were no longer the Greenhawks. Suddenly we are twelve men looking at reality from twelve different angles with twelve different sets of viewing equipment. Fights are starting to erupt. I go to bed one night after a six- or seven-hour hassling session feeling so disgusted about everything that I pin a note on my curtain saying FUCK OFF. In the morning there is yelling in the galley, and Darnell is shaking me and saying, "This one is getting out of hand – you'd better get up." Stagger into the galley with the FUCK OFF sign pinned on my T-shirt. Every day there seems to be some new data-point that has just been picked up by phone or radio, and every new nugget of information seems to have the power to transform the situation entirely. We hassle endlessly about its meaning, throw out ideas about its value, substance, importance, reliability, how it will affect *this* if *that* were to happen, how if *that* got changed, what do we do about *those* and *these*? The galley table is the battleground. Like generals we gather around it and fight over strategy, and we are odd generals, for we are the soldiers in the troop ship that is moving about on the map (pray for the day all wars are fought that way!). And now the

Simmons enraged. Reflected in the mirror is Metcalfe.

terrible question comes up: why are we arguing like this? What are our motives? Egoism? Idealism? Obsession? Or cool calculated practical politics? Ahab or Ishmael? Who is the prime ego? Or is there a prime ego? We are a little band of guerrillas, Captain Cormack's Lonely Hearts Club Band waiting for a Che to emerge.

From the beginning, Bohlen has insisted that he would not be the leader, yet in the early stages we allowed Bohlen and Metcalfe to make the decisions, if only because they seemed like natural leaders. But under their leadership we blundered into the customs hassle at Akutan, and now we are all awakening to the responsibility of assuming our own leadership.

Bohlen is as complex as mirrors mounted opposite each other, each reflecting a reflection of the reflection of the reflection, like an endless series of doors opening into other doors, down down down with no end. America is his nemesis – he hates it like a man who would be a saint hates his own impulse to be a demon. There are fine ironies in this situation for Bohlen. At one point in his career, he solved the intricate materials problem that allowed the Monsanto Company to build its all-plastic House of the Future at Disneyland in 1957. Now he wants to smash America. He also worked for a time for the Hercules Company in Princeton, New Jersey, fabricating the materials for the rocket engines of the Polaris and Minutemen ICBMS, and he worked on the motors of a system – then secret – to be known as the Sprint. By 1971 the Sprint was famous as part of the Anti-Ballistic Missile System, and the test at Amchitka was as closely related to the ABMS as the Sprint had once been. At the very least, Bohlen is a man capable of changes. His psyche is a bio-electronic I Ching. To have come from the middle of the machinery of the military-industrial complex to this funky old boat in an attack on his former masters is no minor fluctuation. And though he seemed determined to let the decision be thrashed out by the group, he has had the final say, for he is the only member of the

Don't Make a Wave Committee actually on board the boat, and as such he controls the purse strings. If he says "Turn around," Captain John will turn around, otherwise he might forfeit his charter fee. Yet Bohlen seems to be straining to keep the options open, so that the main task is to convince him. To this end, Simmons, Fineberg, and I come down solidly on one side, Metcalfe comes down on the other, Bohlen stays in the middle, and the others seem uncertain. In one of his last dispatches from Sand Point, Metcalfe said:

> [The crew of the *Greenpeace*] know that soon, very soon, they'll have to decide whether they should try to wait out bureaucratic delays of the Amchitka test and take the risk of being plowed under the sands of time. . . . If they do decide to go home, they will have failed only on one point. They will have failed to persuade Prime Minister Trudeau to make a personal appeal to President Nixon in Washington. This will be a rather bitter failure for them, because, while they never dreamed that they could stop the Amchitka test themselves, they did believe that Mr Trudeau would eventually come through with his own personal protest. . . . [But] he has not grasped his nettle. If anything, Mr Trudeau has become an accomplice to the bureaucratic delay in Washington. So now the *Greenpeace* must contemplate its own nettle. Whether they grasp it will depend to some extent on whether their voyage was planned as a practical protest to help raise public opinion in Canada or whether it was a hero-trip for the gratification of a few egos. I think I can report confidently now that it was rarely, if ever, a hero-trip, and is in little danger of lapsing into one on the frontier of frustration.

Which few egos was Metcalfe referring to? Well, there is Simmons' ego, and Fineberg's ego, and Hunter's ego. We are a strange alliance: the two American academics and a Canadian who dropped out in high school to write books, falling by accident into the position of Establishment press columnist. Simmons and Fineberg are brilliant at their trade – virtually every argument they put forward is valid – but neither is built for speed. Both move their idea pieces out one by one, starting with the pawns and building toward the play when they pounce with their Queens of Logic. Everything has to go step by step. Nothing can be rushed. And in the end, it is all they can do not to unleash a long howl of I Told You So. Both of them live in the agonizing world of being right, but nobody can stand to listen to the unfolding of their cases.

By contrast, my mind seldom trudges – it bounds and skips through star-beds of ideas. I am more like Moore, a metaphysician of high ecology. When I'm up, I'm very very up, and when I'm down, I'm demolished. "You know," Metcalfe growled at me one afternoon, "the trouble with you is, I can never tell what space your head's in. It keeps moving all over the place." Ego. No doubt about it: *Hunter has ego.* Maybe I'm not so different from John Cormack – I can say the word "defeat," but can I tolerate it? To the others it must seem that I have abandoned my observer role entirely and have become the spokesman for the three-man rebel faction that wants to plunge on to Amchitka come hell or high water. What do they see as my motive? For years I have been strangling in my own torrents of written rhetoric, and I am sick to death of writing propaganda against industrial growth, arms races, racism, and environmental ruin. Now, finally, a rare and welcome opportunity has arisen to confront the Megamachine head-on. Am I an iron radical, or am I more like Don Quixote? Out on the Gulf one afternoon, with the wind screeching and the boat flip-flopping around wildly, somebody noticed that the Canadian flag was being torn to ribbons, but it was stuck – no one could pull it down. When no

Darnell.

one was looking, I sneaked out and climbed to the top of the rigging. One moment I was looking down at the decks, and the next moment I swung far out over the streaming waves. The ladder on the rigging was broken in several places, the rope itself old and frayed, and at the top, I had to stretch my arm to the limit to untangle the flag and rip it free. When I finally made it down, Bohlen looked at me, shook his head, and said: "Now we know what kind of a guy you are. You're a crazy bastard who'll do anything." Yeah. I once wrecked my spine taking a parachute jump without any training, and I have risked my life a hundred times for no good reason. I am either a wild man or driven, and I have been operating on shithouse karma for as long as the *Phyllis Cormack* has. But I am still alive and, apart from a permanently fucked-up back, still in one piece.

WEDNESDAY, OCTOBER 13, 1971

By the time Bohlen calls a meeting for October 12, which turns out to be the Last Meeting, positions have hardened, consensus is hopeless, the crew have polarized, the magic seems dead. There are no miracles in the air, no synchs. The Merry Men in their green uniforms have been reduced to the dreary old gambits of lobbying and hassling, just like a political convention – the party racked by internal divisions, everyone struggling to keep up the appearance of a united front. The last few meetings have deteriorated into shouting matches and new forms of parliamentary style have evolved. Some workers down at the cannery gave us a paper hat with WAKEFIELD'S ALASKA KING CRAB printed on it, and to keep some order in the debate, we agreed that whoever was wearing the KING CRAB hat, and whoever had got hold of the microphone connected to Metcalfe's ever-present tape recorder, had the floor. Back and forth KING CRAB has been passed. Eloquent speeches have been

Metcalfe's turn to speak, as wearer of the WAKEFIELD'S KING CRAB hat.
Bohlen listens.

made beneath it. If you could remove yourself from last night's meeting for a moment and look in from outside, you'd find a delightfully surreal scene – grown men lunging for the microphone and the hat, each new speaker slamming KING CRAB on his head as he opened his mouth. By the Last Meeting, the KING CRAB hat is torn to tatters and we are using a Wakefield's hair net as the speaker's cap. On the table in the middle of everything sits Williwaw, a cat that some local freaks donated and that has no tail, the tiny paper-and-toothpick geodesic dome perched like a sailor's cap on his head. Who are these hairy bleary characters passing a hair net back and forth and shouting at each other? Battered typewriters lie on the floor under the table, clipboards and notes are spread out among the coffee cans and ketchup and sugar cubes and jam and honey cans – all opened the right side up.

The dozen wetsuits have come and gone. The people back home finally found a diving supply house in Vancouver that would lend us the wetsuits for free, and made complicated arrangements to ship them to Sand Point. When they arrived, it turned out there was a customs hangup – we would have to pay $400 duty on them. We didn't have the money, so the whole pack of a dozen wetsuits got shipped back.

And now we are into the final hassle, which revolves around the question of the "executive decision" – that is, Who's the real boss around here? It is Bohlen. Metcalfe says that the executive committee is ultimately responsible to make the decision, "in case the consensus is not a viable and practical consensus. . . . For instance, if the boat was entirely filled with . . . ah . . . ah . . . ah . . . psychedelic kamikaze nuts, you know, who would sail on regardless of the money, regardless of the ability of the ship to do it, regardless of the practical factors." Simmons agrees that we are not going to get a consensus. He asks a theoretical question: if the executive decides to take the boat back to Vancouver, "What is the potential for a mutiny – quote, unquote – and charging on anyway?" Metcalfe says that the executive will preserve "the

Hunter.

Greenpeace idea, ship, concept, funds, charter, etc., etc., . . . as a major tool to awaken the interest and opinion of Canada, and possibly of the United States and the rest of the world, against the Amchitka bomb." Simmons says that the Amchitka voyage is more of a protest voyage than a propaganda voyage, and that it has failed – the proof being the fact that we are talking about whether or not to go home. "If we were really protestors," he says, "we would have no question in our minds which direction to go, strictly on a moral and honest point of view."

I say that if an order was given to go to point x, and suddenly in mid-course the captain said no, and the crew decided to go on to point x, I wouldn't call it a mutiny. I would say that the mutiny had happened on the bridge.

"The *Greenpeace* going to meet the Cannikin of October 2 is different from the *Greenpeace* going to meet the Cannikin of November 2," says Bohlen. "And other differences have been introduced into our situation. For instance, an astounding success in relation to publicity. . . . And the added factor of weather, and added knowledge of this particular ship from a maintenance and operating and mechanical point of view. We're talking about two different trips."

Moore says that a protest in a vacuum is stupid and meaningless, that the purpose of the voyage is to raise awareness. Fineberg points out that we are bound to "peak out" in the day-to-day headlines, and then what? "When you talk about propaganda, you're talking about a complex thing, and it's not each headline in the morning newspaper, it's the people you reach by the example of what you're doing – that they may be reached by our dedication to the mission and they may not be reached by the headline. When it comes down to whether a person will bomb a dam or lobby for a park or a forest. . . . This is a long-term and a subtle thing, not the same as a front-page headline for a week or two."

Keziere brings the discussion back to specifics. He says that if we

Birmingham.

find out the test is absolutely not going to happen in October, we should go back to Vancouver.

"Beyond that," he says, "I think that we have definitely fulfilled our obligation and we would be superfluous in staying out here."

I weigh in as spokesman for the psychedelic kamikaze lunatic fringe, saying that to turn this boat around and go home is certainly to piss away our potential for further success, to stop and say: we've done this much, it's enough, no further, let's go back. None of us could predict the support that has developed as we continued, things like the 10,000 children, so how can we say that we've actualized our potential?

Bohlen says that when we left, a lot of people thought we were loonies, and we proved we weren't loonies, and now we stand a chance of becoming loonies if we go from Sand Point to Amchitka and back to Sand Point in late October and early November in this particular boat. Moore says we would be foolhardy to venture out in this particular weather. Keziere thinks it would be a mistake to turn around because of the *possibility* of bad weather.

"What happened to the idea of going back to Kodiak?" Birmingham asks. "Some people need to get off this boat at the end of October, regardless." He proposes that we go to Kodiak and thin out the crew to five or six men, then proceed. Then he says flatly: "I think there's several members of this crew've definitely made up their minds they're not going to Amchitka come hell, high water, or anything else. Furthermore, the boat is much safer with six men than it is with twelve."

When Birmingham drops his gosh-darn-blankety-blank-old-geezer act and gets around to saying his piece, he is almost always right on. Some guys have made up their minds not to go to Amchitka, so do we split the crew and let those who want to keep on going go, and the rest head home? That is the real question.

This morning, the morning after, as we stand on the dock in the rain and prepare to head home, I say to myself: you lost because Bohlen didn't trust you. Intellectually you're as powerful as him, but you're too much of a freak. He feels he has responsibility for everybody's lives and he will only pass on control to someone whose judgement and maturity he trusts completely. You were doing a lot of crazy things, I point out to myself. Like going around ordaining everybody as a minister in the Greenpeace Church just because you had accidentally become a minister of the Universal Life Church down in some psychedelic place in San Francisco where madmen like Leary hang out. Like the rest of us, Bohlen could see that it was fun, but you did it with the crew of the *Confidence* and with everybody up on Akutan Mountain, man. And then there was that night when those liberal teachers up at the Sand Point School invited the whole crew over for wine, and you and Thurston came staggering in late from the bar, and you took one look at the bookshelf, saw some innocuous children's books of prayers and stuff, and you said, "Who's the Jesus freak around here?" Then you started arguing with them that what the world needed was a religion that took the logical step beyond Christianity into a kind of Eco-Catholicism. Remember when you got back to the boat, and Metcalfe said he'd been waiting for you to show them your stigmata? You jabbering away about Teilhard de Chardin and Marshall McLuhan – it was hard to tell whether you were kidding or serious, man. A flower is your brother. A crab is your brother. A whale is your brother. I am the Earth, we are the Earth, always with a capital *E,* the way other people say "God." Then you disappear into the fog after that trip up Akutan Mountain and we have to go look for you and there you are, clutching your notebook, writing "PARANOID GRANDIOSITY IS THE HUMAN SOUL," and – what was that other beauty? – "I'VE BEEN SANE AND I'VE BEEN INSANE AND BELIEVE ME, INSANE IS BETTER." And you wonder why Bohlen has doubts about your fucking head? When you wanted to be, you were completely sane in the way that Bohlen recognizes sanity. But the rest of the time you must have seemed pretty weird indeed. Like your legalize suicide idea. "It's not enough to lower the birth rate, you've got to raise the death rate. Why not take over from nature? Introduce death control as well as birth control." By taking the stigma out of dying, you said. Encourage people to choose their own time and place of dying. Make it a celebration like birth is a celebration, all the friends gathering around and maybe stoned, whatever they want, go up to the top of a beautiful mountain – "Death is just another trip." Then there was the Greenpeace Church business. The only force that ever threw over empires without arms was religion, you said, and now it would be a scientifically valid religion, based squarely on principles derived from the science of ecology. Make terracide a crime, you said. Some of this made sense and Bohlen even joined in, but you've got to admit that the Hash Cookie Pact was too much. Really, man – that when we die, we get cremated and instead of throwing the ashes to the winds, you bake them into a batch of hash cookies, and your friends have a hash cookie wake and get stoned on the essence of you. Bohlen didn't trust Fineberg and he didn't trust Simmons, so that left you and Metcalfe. If Metcalfe had wanted to go on, Bohlen would have trusted him to take on the leadership. But Metcalfe was pushing harder than any of us to bring the thing to a head, and he was the guy presenting all the arguments for going back. Metcalfe approached the situation at a practical political level. He's been involved in public relations and election campaigns, and those things are real to him. He lived mostly among liberals, and they ran for public office and they controlled the show. From his experience of how power actually operates in a democracy, his practical experience, he fought the Amchitka fight the way you would sell toothpaste. He and Bohlen didn't chicken out. They've both been through heavier trips than you, man. Who wanted to go ahead? Thurston thought the boat should go on and everybody who had to leave could split, which included him. Cummings said his vote was to go home, then he bugged out down into the engine room to write a story or something. Cormack didn't have a vote, but remember that exquisite moment when we had fought it down to the last quivering arm-wrestle, and everybody was wiped out, and Cormack came in and – right, that was your fatal manoeuvre. His opinion was bloody critical, and you knew that he couldn't admit defeat, that he'd come out balls-on, say, "We can make it. There's not a damn thing wrong with this boat. This's the finest sea boat on the whole coast. She'll take you anywhere. Ain't no kind of weather this boat can't handle!" You had it all figured out – Cormack's confidence would turn the tide. But what you didn't count on was that after he'd finished his little speech – which came out exactly as you'd guessed – he'd add, in a desperate tone of voice if there ever was one, *"But you'd be crazy to try it!"* So we wound up with Darnell, Simmons, Fineberg, and you willing to keep on going. That's all. You lost. I had the feeling that there was a part of you that wanted to lose, a feeling of *My God, I can't get my arm up to swing again. I'm running out of punches.* Maybe you even knew that Cormack's act wouldn't hold up, that he'd betray himself. In fact, I think you threw the fight. Very clever – you do the balls-on trip all the way, and then when the whole thing balances on a pin, you cleverly allow yourself to be beaten. And wow! At the end you come out the hero in that damn book you knew all along you were going to write, and the other guys are the heavies. But wait. Let me take all that shit back. That night after the vote was over, you said, "Well, all I have to say . . . is. . . ." And then you made this animal noise and literally flew up from the table and went through the galley door so hard you broke the hinge off, and you went out to the stern and cried. If that was an act, it was damn convincing. Then everybody went down to the bar and drank till God knows when. And that weird synch! At midnight, when you looked up and said, "Well, congratulate me. It's October 13. As of now, I'm thirty years old." Talk about turning into a pumpkin, man! That was delicious. But by that time you'd lost your sense of humour.

Was it ever easy to tell who was the winner and who was the loser, that night in the bar. You were coming apart at the seams.

What is it Metcalfe said? "Never let anyone tell you this is an ego trip – it's an ego *trap*." Every minute of this experience has been so fucking intense – to be so alive is to realize how dead we are normally. Is that a justification for wars and fighting? When people are struggling like that, when they're out of their snug little boxes – which are traps, they really are – and into some life-or-death action, there's a payoff. They do come alive. They experience everything much more intensely and at many more levels. If people could wake up from those stale little situations they're in, and stay awake, there really would be a revolution. You get a taste of it, of being alive, being in a struggle, being a part of a vast and positive fight for survival – that's what it's about. Survival on a bigger-than-me scale.

The God is dead business. Yeah, He is dead. And we miss Him, we really do. Because when God is dead, it's a tricky thing to keep meaning alive. That's what's happening in the West. God died and the people were afraid. God took the beautiful dream of immortality away with Him and left us nothing but the void. Timidly people began to feel their way into the void. At about that time, the East and the West began to move into a new stage of harmony. And through the science of ecology, the techniques of systems analysis, the media of mass communications, and existential and phenomenological philosophies, a consciousness has begun rapidly to evolve that can think in terms of wholes instead of parts, that can see the world as a single life system vibrant in the vastness of the cosmos. The Princess Immortality was not taken away by God in his dying. The people were simply blinded and so could not perceive Her in the Earth, in every drop of rain. In the fear of dying was the invention of God, and in the dying of God was the chance to shake off the fear of going back into the Earth to nourish Her and to go on being, in however transmuted a form. God is dead. Long live the Earth!

Hunter on his thirtieth birthday at the bar in Sand Point, Alaska.

Out past the Sand Point wharf, past the grocery store and the little white wooden liquor store, around the peninsula whose tip is the cannery, there is a small hidden bay. Winds come steadily over the far slope and beat at the tall grass, ribbons grey on one side and rinsed-out autumn yellow on the other, rust-hued goldenrod, tumbleweeds caught like giant gangly insects in barbed wire, knocked-down fence posts riddled with termite holes – a scene right out of the rolling hills of old Montana or a lagoon valley on the Saskatchewan prairie in late fall. Old shacks half-hidden in the hushing and shooshing grass, as high as your chest in places, and up on the slope a cluster of rusting Quonset huts. Garbage piled up, old grey nets, a few weathered wooden swings moving in the wind, as though invisible children were pensively swinging on them. Cold – the wind has winter cold in it. Huskies yap from the ends of their ropes, but the sound is carried away on the wind. No sound except for the rare *splap tssssshhh* of waves being beaten into the bay, a few ancient rowboats clacking together along the gravel beach, and the *skrik skrik* of tires rubbing the ribs of boats at the little wharf, like an overturned box. In hushes, in breaths that envelop sound, the wind streams down into the cove around the bay. An object very much like a totem pole pushes up clear of the tall waving grass at the top of the rise against the sky – another Russian Orthodox Church. Its windows are all broken and the bottom bar of the double cross has tilted, creating a new religious sign, a whole new denomination. This old heap on the edge of the ghost town ghetto represents perhaps the farthest reaches of the Russian Orthodox Church (in town, all the metaphysical action is down at the Baptist Hall), and now it is a chess piece, a bishop, abandoned in enemy territory. The place is some kind of historic site, though nobody has put a plaque there yet. In the cemetery around the church, small saplings grow between the gravestones. The decks of the empty boats in the bay squeak as the ghosts of old fishermen still walk them, the huskies bark silently, unseen children brood on the swings. . . .

I have wandered down into the cove a dozen times, but almost never have I glimpsed any figure moving among the Quonset huts and the hunkered-down windblown shacks, and no one at all climbing over the old hulks around the dock. Every day the sky is a soiled sheet laid over too many corpses. One small gillnetter is beached on the dirty gravel, a splintering bone of a boat, windows smashed, hull like the wrappings of a mummy – the funkiest old place in the world you could imagine for kids to have their secret clubhouse, a place to duck out of the wind and listen to it hissing through the old rust-scabby engine like a primitive Moog synthesizer left there by an ancient forgotten race. That old boat is a cold spooky sad place to take shelter in, but Thurston and Keziere and I fell in love with it as soon as we saw it, not long after we got to Sand Point. Years ago, somebody painted the word LOU on the hull, in green. Lou is also the name of the girl Keziere is living with, and Thurston and I have gotten to know Lou just well enough that we love her too. That boat is mysteriously cool and together, and it possesses the Secret Wisdom, like the wisdom of mature beautiful women, which has no real counterpart in the world of men. Lovingly, we crowded into the *Lou* and Keziere warmed himself on the invoked presence of his Lou. Best of all, with the same green paint someone had sloshed a crude peace symbol and the word PEACE on the hull. Here was another *Greenpeace,* here was the wreck of the *Greenpeace,* here finally was the past and the future spirit of the *Greenpeace* – a deep-sinking feeling, for the end is so certain, death can be beautiful, don't be afraid to go back into the vibrant voids out of which all "things" come into brief focus or brief out-of-focus. In its wise graceful ancestral way, the *Lou* seemed a finer totem pole-like return to the beginning than even the old chess piece of a Russian Orthodox church up on the hill.

Today, the day after the vote to give up the assault on Amchitka, I walk to town to buy an airline ticket that will get me out of here, moving blindly in a fog of pain and self-loathing, thinking Greenpeace is dead, *Greenpeace is dead,* I am dead, we are all dead, *we are all dying.* But Thurston and Keziere head me off and march me down to the *Lou.* We sit there smoking for a long while and we seem to be on-board the real *Greenpeace,* the death ship of the vision and the dream. After a while, one by one we begin to laugh . . . and laugh . . . and cry . . . and laugh. This is the real Greenpeace trip, sailing in a bone-boat sarcophagus across waving prairie badlands of grass, winter light pressing down through the ragged hole torn in the roof, the boat listing as though frozen in a moment when it took a wave over the bow. All we can see through the empty sockets of the windows is winter light and the soiled shroud coming down once again over sea and Earth and men with their crazy ambitions. Heaving upward in a moment of eternal sea riding, we are beached and peeling and broken, we are sitting in pews in a haunted church of our own, the wind playing the rusting engine like an organ. It is a fine long staring into the grave of our hope, it is a fine deep hurt, it is a fine dark voyage we take, Thurston, Keziere, and I, the broken wrecked old boat, broken wrecked old dream, broken wrecked old heads of ours.

When we pull away from Sand Point in the afternoon, the only people to see us off are three local freaks who stand on the dock waving at us, moments after having sadly handed down to us a sign they had painted on a plank: GREENPEACE IS A BUMER [*sic*]. I sit on the Picasso-like winch, riding it like a supermarket camel, wielding a cigarette holder made of a crab claw. I am stupefied and dazed – we are all dazed – and the only thing I can hear myself saying is: "Responsibility is absolute."

The Gulf of Alaska, October.

Home

The long blank numb retreat from Sand Point. The boat is like a museum in the late afternoon. All the energy has been spent, has blown through the rooms of the boat like the wind leaving a ruin. A museum. An air of decay. Up until the moment we finally splintered, broke, and turned around, a thrumming tension had passed through us all, a constant state of bracing oneself for the confrontations that always lay ahead. It was like bracing oneself to lift a great rock, only to step back from it and walk away. The body whines. The mind bursts loose with tracers of stored-up pumped-up ready-to-fire energy, all dissipating uselessly into thin air. The flames we stoked to hold us at the gate now come flickering like sparks that we dash in each other's faces as we wound one another with our remarks. Humour, which has always been the truest language, now cuts like snakebites. Fineberg left the boat at Sand Point and flew back to Anchorage, saying he could do more there. Simmons decided against leaving and I was talked out of it. But it was right for Fineberg to go. "I believe I got scapegoated for raising the questions I raised," he said. "I got kicked in the teeth for trying as best I knew how to do what we all said we were trying to do – protest Cannikin. It's a heavy trip to work through."

Chugging south from Sand Point, we have nothing to do but work it through. Down down down we sink, the weather rough all the way, barbs shooting back and forth, psychological wrestling matches going on at every level. Thurston is Doc Doom, making insane babbling speeches like a maniac raving in a mirror. He glides, he squirms, he plays along the jagged edges of the void wherein the mind can lose itself forever. He speaks like a phony schoolteacher, a petty official, Lucy in "Peanuts," your most boring uncle, a suburban lady at a cocktail party, on and on through legions of stereotypes. He has them down pat because he sees through them like wraiths. He knows their every number, their every act, their every routine, and routinely he turns those blazing x-ray eyes of his on the rest of us and cuts through our acts and games with surgical precision. On the wooden fridge door is pinned a radiogram, dated October 12, 1971:

MASTER AND CREW GREEN PEACE

PHYLLIS CORMACK (AT HARBOR SAND POINT ALASKA)

THE VANCOUVER MEETING OF THE RELIGIOUS SOCIETY OF

FRIENDS SENDS LOVING WISHES FOR A SUCCESSFUL AND

SAFE MISSION. WE SUPPORT YOU IN YOUR COURAGEOUS

EFFORT TO STOP THE AMCHITKA BLAST AND TO HELP TURN

THE WORLD TOWARD HUMAN GOALS.

MARGARET LORENZE CLER.

Across it, in ballpoint, somebody has scribbled: COWARDLINESS IS NEXT TO GODLINESS.

Moore slumps at the table, gurgling with silent wiped-out laughter. This laughter is pain. I have never seen so clearly the connection between laughter and the moans and gasps of agony – even ordinary laughter, come to think of it, people moaning and crying out in front of one another, everybody hypnotized into believing that those squeaks and *huk huk huks* are fun noises and everything is okay. We are into another movie, one without season or weather, without colour or shape, without aim or purpose. Do you think your vision is perfect? No. Then it must be distorted. I guess you're right. So everything you see and believe to be true is false. It can't be helped. Down down down like bubbles we sink.

Then, as we approach Kodiak, a motorboat comes out to guide us in and a crowd stands on the dock with a big sign saying THANK YOU GREENPEACE, and people are waving and cheering, and there, perched at the very of the dock, grinning up at us through his ragged dog-hair beard, is Rod Marining, the non-leader of the northern lunatic fringe of the Youth International Party, better known as the Yippies, shaking his head, wearing an old weather-beaten leather jacket, tape recorder slung over his shoulder, headphones around his neck. "Boy, I don't know about you guys!" he yells. "You look weird – you look like spooks, man! You really do!" All along, it has been one of the finer fantasies of the voyage that Marining will suddenly show up, riding a whale or sitting on the deck of a passing fishing boat. For Marining, the year has been an endless spiral of busts, demonstrations, border blockades, near-riots, and hassles with the cops. That is the regular routine of a Yippie – one day liberating land about to be grabbed by real estate sharks and setting up a people's park, a few days later protesting French nuclear testing, the day after that constructing a twelve-foot joint of marijuana to be passed around to the crowd at a mass smoke-in – but in spite of that busy summer, Rod has managed to show up for almost every meeting of the Don't Make a Wave Committee. At one point he even tried to buy his own little boat in which to sail to Amchitka. His plan was to levitate the island, cast voodoo spells on the bomb, broadcast an appeal for help to Namor, Prince of Atlantis, call in Aquaman, and pull a host of other mad Yippie media tricks. He had painted the big peace and ecology symbols on our sail and had worked furiously at various joe jobs in the hope that he might come with us. But some members of the Committee had opposed it. Right to the moment when the boat pulled away from the dock at Vancouver, Marining was there, yelling to us as we chugged away, "Wait! You'll see! I'll be on the boat! I just know it, man. See you later!" I, for one, have not doubted for a minute that somehow, sometime, against all odds, Marining would end up on the boat.

And here he is at Kodiak, grinning away, and now there is a spare bunk, and at least one vision is not yet smashed – Marining's mystical vision that he will board the *Greenpeace*. We are heading in the wrong direction, but he'll be on-board. It turns out he flew to Prince Rupert after we left, betting that somebody would get too seasick to continue and leave the boat at that point, whereupon he'd come aboard. When we didn't stop at Prince Rupert, he flew back to Vancouver and took part in border blockades. Then he hitchhiked to Seattle, took a plane to Anchorage and hitchhiked from there to Kodiak, arriving just in time to stir up publicity and organize a welcoming committee. It took a certain amount of guts to hitchhike across Alaska, where only a year ago a hippie was beaten up so badly he lost both eyes. Naturally we take Marining aboard.

THURSDAY, OCTOBER 21, 1971

We spend three days in Kodiak, attending public meetings and giving speeches against Cannikin. Coast Guard types lay little presents on us, and the police chief sends us an Alaska flag to fly alongside the Greenpeace flag. A local Greenpeace Committee gets set up, local liberal press people come down to cover the event, anti-Cannikin feeling is everywhere, the police chief raises a toast to us at a dinner being held in our honour (*our* honour? What's going on?), and Marining sits there in his calm serene spaced-out fashion, nodding and smiling at the Chief of Police. Alaskan congressmen and congresswomen and a woman senator show up at the public meetings, and we descend from the pure crystalline heights of an international life-or-death protest to a troupe of party politicians making speeches. Again and again Bohlen gets up in front of a room packed with Alaskans and, as tirelessly as an actor on *Sesame Street*, explains the dangers with every letter of the alphabet, starting with A for arms race, B for bombs in general, C for Cannikin in particular, D as in Doomsday, E for environment. . . . Right about here, sick to death of listening to Bohlen go through the whole song and dance of educating people about the obvious, I am forcing myself not to jump up and yell, "F for fuck the bastards!" I settle for heckling him with in-jokes that can only be understood by the crew. The Alaskans don't get the jokes. They just frown and look uncomfortable that one of these good guys is such a weirdo.

A piece of graffiti on the wall of the Kodiak meeting hall is so appropriate that I want to shout it aloud to the audience, mainly local politicians, teachers, concerned citizens, concerned parents, idealistic youth, journalists, and members of the Alaska Mothers' Campaign Against Cannikin: SOME PEOPLE I KNOW ACT SO FUCKED UP, THEY NEED TO BE SHOT. Then a round of receptions and another meeting. The Greenhawks find themselves in the home of a Gestalt therapist whose wife is throwing the I Ching for Thurston as Cormack sits in a plush chair, sipping wine, surrounded by incredibly beautiful young women, mostly teachers, social workers, and psychiatrists. There on the wall, our host has tacked up a truth:

> Whatever has been, has been
> Whatever must be, shall be
> Whatever can be, may be
> Whatever I was, I was
> Whatever I must be, I will be

Whatever I can be, I may be
But whatever I am – I am

We find out that shortly after the incident with the *Confidence,* both the Coast Guard and the Navy issued orders forbidding any of their men to fraternize with us. The brass imposed fines on the entire crew of the *Confidence,* and three junior officers – the three who had been on the launch? – were demoted. But nobody would take their jobs, so they had to be reinstated. Oh, the American military machine is in a state of disarray.

Now we are out on the Gulf of Alaska, swinging more than 200 miles out from land, toward Juneau, where the Governor of Alaska is reported to be waiting to greet us as a gesture of solidarity with the anti-Amchitka forces. Potentially this is an important political move, as it may put more pressure on Nixon to cancel the test. The waves are coming up high and the grey pastes of cloud that flew away from us along the horizon yesterday are backing up now and bearing down on us like dark bruises, their sails rimmed with throbbing flares. "See them clouds up ahead?" Cormack said when they were still running away. "That's the storm that's just passed. It's moving away about seventy, maybe eighty miles an hour, and we're just poking along about nine knots behind 'er. Wal, long as she keeps moving that way, we're okay. Nuttin' coming up behind us so far as we know. Only thing we have to worry about is if them clouds up ahead turn around and start headin' for us. We're pretty far out. Cape St Elias is about, wal, pretty near 250 miles over that way. . . ." Marining just stood there smiling serenely, seeming to hear what Cormack is saying even though the headphones are still fixed firmly over his ears and we knew he was listening to the Joe Cocker version of "With a Little Help From My Friends" recorded at Woodstock.

Marining bugs the skipper something awful. When he first came aboard and sat down in the galley with the headphones on, Cormack took one look at him and snorted, "What's that? A spaceman?" Absolutely right on, John! Marining is a spaceman. A very spaceman. After only two nights at sea, Cormack ordered him out of the radio room. "Goddamn goony bird! Sleeps there on the floor 'stead of the bunk. A man can't goddamn move without tripping all over that goddamn goony bird lying there like a big stupid bug with goddamn space things on his head." If some of the rest of us are a bit hard for Cormack to take, we are solid citizens in comparison to Marining. To top it all off, he has one startlingly dark brown eye and one seashell-glittering grey eye. You can go quietly mad talking to him, for if you look him in the brown eye, he is one person, but if you shift your gaze slightly to look into his grey eye, he is another person. He knows perfectly well what an advantage that gives him over other people. Just by staring back at you he can break your grip on certainty and even sanity, depending on how strong your grip was to begin with. Marining is weird, all right – too weird for Cormack. He has taken to defending himself in the most devastating manner – by looking back at Cormack, not saying a thing, just letting his two different eye-personas have their effect. Now he says, "Getting a little rough, ain't she, skipper?" Cormack ignores him and keeps his eye fixed on the sky. He's jittery. Keeps rubbing his china and muttering to himself. I am tempted to ask him, "Is *this* fuck-all, John?" But the old boy doesn't look like he's in much of a mood for wisecracks. Down in the galley, Moore is saying, "Cormack's really uptight. We must be in for it. Oh Jesus."

Bohlen has recovered his vital impish quality. Metcalfe has stirred from his bunk and is looking out through the open door over the poop deck, lime green water washing like a flood from a broken dam across the open space between the forecastle and the battenclaim. "That figures," Thurston mutters. "If there was any time when we'd get killed, for sure it would happen on the way home. Fuck *around.*

We won't even get to be heroes." There is such perverse logic in that comment that I start to think, yeah, this is probably it. Once we were actually retreating, we were all in such a rush to get back home that we had pressured Cormack like hell to speed it up. Maybe he was tired and fed up too. Whatever the reason, he decided to take a little chance. Now that the Gulf is being swept by winter storms, he should have avoided going out into its deeps. We could have followed the Inside Passage all the way back, skipping from the lee of one island to the lee of the next, always within sight of coves where we could take shelter.

We took that approach once between Sand Point and Kodiak. Cormack pulled into a cove beside a little island to duck out of a squall, and four other Canadian fishing boats had holed up there as well. All the skippers knew each other and they yakked over their radios and exchanged gossip and rumours. A few crewmen from one of the other boats came over in a punt and gave us some skin books in return for a bottle of wine. The wind cried like a giant gull, and gusts smacked the waters of the cove, making the sail go *whap* and the whole boat lurch. The anchor was down and some of the other boats had even let down their stabilizers. Like wet animals we cowered together, five bobbing chained boats in the crying wind. Late in the afternoon, a voice crackled through the radio. One of the boys hadn't found his way out of the open water yet. There was a held-back thrill of horror in the man's voice: "Nuttin' on the radar yet. Maybe she ain't workin'." Then one of the other captains here in the safety of the cove would call out through the *skrawks* and *sssssssssts* of static: "Wind changed yet?" *Ssssssssst . . . ooooooweeeeeeeee.* "Not much. Still nor'west." *Urp whurp whurp ooooooweeeeeeeeeeee.* "Took a green one over the stern there. . . ." Sounds come through the radio like saw blades in slow motion, notes so high they hurt. Half a dozen of us crowd up in the radio room, Metcalfe taping the whole thing. Birmingham explains that that's really bad news, taking a green one over the stern, because the ass end's not built to handle the impact of that many tons of water hitting right on her. *Oyn oyn oyneeeeeiiiiiii whirn whirn whirn.*

"Any change in that wind yet, Hank? You should be picking up Cape Seal any minute." *Eeek eeeeekk ssssssst.*

"Ask him if there's any change in depth yet." *Sssst.*

"Hank? Hank? Y'hear me?"

Eeeeeiiiiiii eeeeiiiiii yi yi yi orrrrrrrrrrrrrrr. . . . "Loud and clear. Over."

"John says what's your depth? If you're where he figures, it should start getting shallow fast."

Urp whurp whurp ssssssssssssssstttttttt. "Still 'bout seventy fathoms. No, wait, she's changin'. Round fifty now."

"Okay, that's good. Cape Seal should be just about dead ahead in a couple of minutes."

It took hours to guide in that lost boat, the *Sleep Robber*, tension spitting through the storms of static, the bird-cries of the wind, the *whap* of the sail. By morning, the storm had let up enough that Cormack could up anchor and make a break for Kodiak.

And now we are out in the open ourselves, 250 miles south of Cape St Elias, in about 3,000 fathoms of water, midway between Kodiak Island and Juneau, no sheltered little coves to duck into, and the storm that swept the Gulf is rolling right back over us. We are starting to take green ones ourselves, and the water is beginning to smoke. Up in the Penthouse we have to hang on with both hands, and so much water has splashed in through the port doorway, which keeps banging open, that even the guy at the wheel goes slipping and sliding around. Sometimes when you cling to the wheel with all your strength, you find your feet on the port wall – the boat is tipping over that far. Nobody can hold the wheel for more than half an hour at a time. There is nothing languid about the *Phyllis Cormack* now. We plunge down the sides of waves like a hundred-ton surfboard, and no longer are we lifted magically on the back of the next wave. The bow smashes the onrushing wall like a battering ram. With each crash, the whole boat shudders. "We're starting to torpedo," Bohlen announces, his voice shivering with that alive feeling that blooms in the face of death. Cormack isn't making any more jokes. We are finally in actual trouble, the wind coming across the hunched shoulders of legions of grey waves in eighty-mile-an-hour blasts. One moment the windows in front of the wheel are translucent ectoplasm, the next they are grey nothingness as we tunnel through a forty-foot mountain of solid water.

Cormack takes the wheel himself and refuses to give it up. He slaps his great belly against the wheel to hold it steady while he grapples for a single spoke with his tree-roots of arms. Then, with a lurch like a man swinging a sledgehammer, he yanks the wheel this way, and that way, and harder that way. *Grunt. Wham. Heave.* "Gotta watch fer the freak ones," he says between grunts. "They're the ones that come up like a pyramid. Like that over there – all green. One of them comes up under the bow a certain way and she can flip ya right over. *Hup! Uhhh!"* The impact of the waves is like being hit by boulders being hurled from below and massive boot-kicks to the hull. "It's cat and mouse now," says Cormack, his eyes scanning the sea for freak ones. He kicks the port door open and sticks his head out into the whistling whining crying keening wind to see whether she's changed direction. He tries plowing straight into the waves, but we are torpedoing. Then he hauls her over to the left and tries taking them at an angle, but we nearly get caught in a couple of those green pyramids that lunge up with no warning. One of them explodes into the sky just off the bow, rattling the boat like a tin can full of dimes. For just a few seconds it feels as though we have left the water and are skidding crazily on ice, then we tumble off, and back into the water. The ocean has transformed itself into a tangle of vast twisting sinews, crushing everything in its path.

Out on deck it is another planet. The air is a baying moaning thing that comes slapping at our faces and smacking our bodies. Metcalfe has become Ernest Hemingway, sitting quietly and sipping his coffee while shells from Krupp cannons crash around him. Bohlen breathes like a man in an icy shower, gasping with the terrible ecstasy of it. Simmons has dug in like a bulldog. When Cormack has to check the engine, pump out the bilge tanks, eat, or crap, Simmons takes his turns at the wheel even though he is being thrown around like a rag doll. Thurston plays Beethoven and Tchaikovsky at full blast on Marining's tape recorder as waves smash against the plexiglass galley windows. Down in the engine room, Cummings rides on a canvas camping chair in front of the typewriter, furiously tapping out descriptions of the storm:

> As the sea built up around us, perceptive Cormack watchers began to sense a subtle change not in his habits, but in his attitude. He still dozed for an hour, had a cup of tea, walked the bridge, looking, sniffing, sensing. But now there was an alertness about him that belied his years and his weight. He seemed to be tuning himself in to the elements more finely than a radar beam on a foggy night. One after another, the crew took their turns at the wheel and tried to follow John's instructions to "keep 'er lined up with the wind." Gradually the sway became a lurch, and then an intricate trapeze of down-right-left-up that turned ship and crew into absurd pantomimes of themselves. Clothes on their hangers swung out like a rubber chorus line, frozen for one, two, three seconds in a horizontal kick before snapping back against the bulkheads. Bodies were lifted half out of bunks then thrown back as if in contempt. Dishes clattered in the galley, turned into a sauna by a suddenly sloshed teapot. On the bridge, the watch hung onto the wheel, trying to keep it and him from being thrown by the tilt. Still, John mostly looked, sniffed, sensed. The hills of water turned

into jagged mountains that would suddenly froth. Then,
green water over the bow . . . the sign that the situation
was getting worthy of concern. The ship had developed a
tendency to reverse itself, to turn around and go broadside
into the waves. At that point, Cormack took over the
wheel. . . . The man and his ship have become compatible
to a degree seldom seen in conventional marriages. His
circumference is almost exactly that of the hatches to the
engine room and the bridge, his eyes are attuned to every
squeak and murmur that should be there and every click
that shouldn't, his feet innately know every board and ridge
from wheelhouse to rope locker. . . .

Moore, Darnell, and Keziere have pretty well retreated to their bunks.
Birmingham hurries back and forth between the engine room and the
Penthouse, having incomprehensible conversations with John about
the bilge tanks and the state of things down in the hold. Marining puts
on his nylon flight jumpsuit, slaps his headphones over his ears, and
climbs out into the wind and waves to groove on the storm. Out on
the bow, he and I get hold of a thick rusty chain, then ride down like
birds, down, down, gargantuan surfboard ride through green flinging-
up mountains and streams of smoky foam, the whole boat crashing
down like a truck dropping from a cliff, and just at the moment when
the bow torpedos into the wave, we pull ourselves up in the air and
swing from the chain, while a whole ocean of water smashes over the
bow, whipping our faces and hands in stinging bites. If we are going
to die, it is going to be a wild ride of a dying. Marining passes me
the headphones between waves, and through the wind and thundering
drum rolls of rising water I am listening to Ten Years After doing their
super-adrenaline-fired Woodstock version of "I'm Going Home."
    And now a dolphin breaks the water like a grey knife, leaping

out just ahead of the bow, flipping itself into the air and looking at us along its dark duck-like mouth. Didn't I read somewhere that dolphins sometimes rescue shipwrecked men floundering in the water? That they swim alongside ships in distress to give sailors moral support? "Hey, dolphin!" yells Marining. "Wanna borrow the headphones?" The dolphin flips into the air again, as if to say, so it's an eighty-mile-an-hour wind and fifty-foot waves – so what? It's heaven. Don't let the fear of death get in your way! We whoop and holler like kids playing on the most incredible carnival ride ever invented, and Cormack watches us from up in the Penthouse, where he is still fighting the wheel. "Pin it with his stomach, spin it back, pin it," writes Cummings. Moore hangs on to the edge of his bunk with one hand and tries to concentrate on *Lord of the Rings* and all of us think about the damn two-by-four down in the engine room, wedged between the big Atlas engine and the hull, possibly the only thing that is keeping the engine from toppling over.

Now the bilge tank pump breaks down and the engine room starts to flood. Cormack is down there cursing and working furiously to fix it. The engine splutters and farts and coughs, making the same noises it made just before it conked out completely a month ago as we crossed the Gulf of Alaska. It was flat calm then, so when the engine went, we just bobbed around like an apple in the swells until Cormack got it fixed. But *now. . . .* Darnell wants to know if everybody has said their morning prayer to the engine god.

"How do we watch out for the freak ones when its gets dark, John?"

He shrugs. "It's a checker game now."

There he is, agile as a cat, a grey-green toque jammed down on his head, torn purple and grey plaid shirt with shredded sleeves, big leather boots, white whiskers prickling out all over his jowls, concentrating like a concert pianist, poised like a surfer, legs bent and braced, steak-sized hands wrapped around the spokes of the wheel, and the years fall away.

The flapping old man is gone, and there is a muscular barrel-chested Hell's Angel of a sea captain, brawling his way across the screaming barroom. It is a sight that makes me want to cry out, "Come on, John!" cheering on the Lone Ranger or the guy leaping into the sky from the phone booth.

But as the hours wear on, even Cormack's cast-iron body begins to tire. He knows that he can't solo this one – sooner or later he's going to have to trust one of these damn amateurs with the wheel. Near the end of the third day out here, after thirty-five hours of the boat chopping away at the waves like an axe, wind like a moan from the void, everybody battered and bruised from being thrown against walls and cupboards and ladders and bunks, enough of us have pumped Cormack for information that we can imagine getting through the storm alive if our skipper passes out or collapses from exhaustion.

That night, the ocean kicks the shit out of us. Cormack rests fitfully in his bunk, getting up again and again to give Bohlen and Simmons fresh instructions. "Feels like she's running stronger this way now, take her over a little more to the left. . . . Keep her there steady 'less you can't keep the wheel up, then let her fall a bit the way she wants to go and try to ease to the right for a while. Sometimes you can kind of zigzag your way through."

By morning, only five of us can still get out of our bunks. Cormack gives the order to swing her around, and Bohlen and I tackle the wheel together, using all of our combined remaining strength to hang on as the boat cracks like a whip and bucks and throws herself over so far that the water looks to be running directly below the port door. If that damn door bangs open now, we'll drop right into the ocean. Incredible long seconds of being shaken like dolls by the convulsing of the wheel as the old boat bounces like a stand-up punching bag with a weight at the bottom. The boat almost – *almost* – goes over, but doesn't, and once we have steadied the wheel again, we are running with the water and an entirely new motion has taken us over. Now we have a following sea, a sea that lifts you like a leaf and wafts you this way and that, raising you lazily, then settling you down as if it were lowering an infant into a bathtub – except that the bathtub is riding around like a horse galloping in slow motion. Ahead of us a path appears like an abandoned trail, and all we have to do is keep the nose of the boat pointed into the trail, while the wind sweeps past in jet streams as low and fierce as a winter blizzard. We can just barely detect a slight absence of streamers directly ahead, like a windprint of the boat – our wake lies ahead of us and we are driving back into it.

"Gotta watch this kind of thing," says Cormack, looking no less uptight than when we were plowing head-on.

"What's the danger now, John?"

"Wal, you get a following sea like this and you don't have to work so hard, if you know what I mean. But you can get caught nappin'. Them waves are still out there, even if you can't feel 'em so much on account of we're not joggin' into 'em any more. But the stern ain't built like the bow, and you don't have to take too many of 'em over the stern before she starts to break up."

So we handle the wheel like a great butterfly, stroking her wings, breathing on her antennae, holding her ever so gently and trying to let the bow flow the way she wants into the wake, making tiny adjustments whenever the ass end swings out too much. We can feel the tons of water being pulled by planetary forces, opening and closing like a vast dark lens at our backs. For a whole day we drift through the angel dance of the following sea, Marining and I chortling over the idea that fate has decided to take a hand in things. Isn't the wind driving us back, directly toward Amchitka? And wouldn't that be the final grand piano, the storm depositing us on the doorstep of Cannikin on the day the beast emerges, clad in its isotopes and Hiroshima glitter? Williwaw, the cat, gets over her seasickness and takes to moving from bunk to bunk, apparently choosing to sleep with whatever guy is feeling the worst.

Eventually the storm sweeps past us. "Hard around!" Cormack barks once more. We churn wildly between the troughs again, then the *Phyllis Cormack* straightens like a gull wing and beings again to whack her axe of a bow into the surges of sea. "Got 'er licked now," Cormack says, and on we sail toward Juneau. Once again we have lived through a storm. The death ship period is over and we are back to laughing and jokes. The skin books that the fishermen gave us have been pulled apart and pages displayed all over the galley in an orgy of sticking up pictures of nubile naked women. Being horny is being alive. The fishermen had also given us some choice tabloids, with headlines like NEW DISCOVERY MAKES YOU A STUD FOREVER, BORED WIVES ACT IN DIRTY MOVIES FOR SEX KICKS, INSIDE A VICE TRAINING SCHOOL, TRIBE DISCOVERS HOW TO STAY VIRILE LONGER — THEY DRINK OWN SPERM! GROUPIE GIVES BIRTH TO QUADRUPLETS — BY FOUR DIFFERENT FATHERS! BOY GIVEN LSD — GOES INSANE! And the classic: COCAINE-CRAZED RATS TERRORIZE BRAZILIAN CITY! We got a few new song lyrics out of those tabloids. "Or would you rather be a cocaine-crazed Brazilian rat?" "Or would you rather be a sperm-drinking stud making dirty movies for sex kicks?" In one of the papers there was a full-page ad for a life-size real-in-every-detail rubber love doll moulded from the bodies of actual Hollywood actresses. We named all the people we'd like to send a rubber love doll to, starting with Richard Nixon and working down through John Wayne and the bosses of the U.S. Atomic Energy Commission.

Into Juneau we come chugging, in the blue tail end of October, glaciers on dark mountains, moonlight on ice, the lights of Juneau coming on like campfires beneath the Arctic cliff-faces. We have heard that there will be some kind of welcoming committee, which may include the Governor, and a town meeting. Cormack has even shaved and decked himself out in his fedora, woollen Sunday jacket, polished black shoes, and grey trousers. But where the hell do we land? Cormack finally picks out a cannery wharf. We pull in, Darnell leaps up from the stern, and we all feel quite pleased with ourselves – if nothing else, we are finally beginning to learn how to dock the boat. But there is no welcoming committee in sight, unless you count the three guys who wander down the dock and yell, "What kind of fish ya bringing in?" Now we see that the wharf is blocked off at both ends of the cannery by high hurricane fence gates, securely locked. "We're closed today," explains one of the guys. Darnell asks them if they've heard anything about a welcome for the *Greenpeace*. Nope, they haven't heard a thing about it. "Ain't you guys bringing in fish? Well, what ya doing then?"

Cormack still has the engine chugging and the rest of us are flopping around on the poop deck laughing at this embarrassingly stupid scene when a couple of young people run up to the hurricane fence and yell, "Hey, *Greenpeace!* You're at the wrong dock! Go back and under the bridge and turn right at the first pier!" Right. Darnell starts to untie the rope, but by now the boat has drifted out too far for him to get back in. " I'll go with those people," he yells, throwing the rope and galloping toward the hurricane fence. But the well-wishers have already disappeared. Darnell turns and runs madly back toward the boat as Cormack tries to throw her into reverse. The boat crushes against the pilings, then bounces back from the dock and wallows around, Darnell dangling from the ladder and reaching out for my hand but not quite connecting. He climbs back up on the dock and runs twenty feet down it while Cormack shouts obscenities at him. Then back he comes charging – "No no, *no!*" everybody is yelling, "don't try it!" – and he sails off the end of the wharf. For a moment it looks as though he's going to fall short and splash into the water, but no, he crashes onto the deck with an awful *thunk*, and Cormack slaps her into gear and away we steam.

The tide is high, and when we pass under the bridge, the masthead and its ornament – the UN flag, now a tattered blue and white rag –

almost scrape the underbelly of the bridge. A small rain-soaked crowd of people wave madly from the first pier, but Cormack doesn't see them. The *Greenpeace* sails on past them, then banks around slowly and takes a good fifteen minutes to angle back in toward the pier with its ring of docked boats. Finally Cormack noses us in, crunching against a crab boat as he goes. Several hundred supportive souls were in attendance three hours ago, when we were supposed to arrive, but by this time the welcoming crowd has dwindled to about a dozen soggy people. The Governor of Alaska has sent a message: "I'm glad you made it back into these waters safely. I admire your courage in carrying out your convictions and I think you have proven your point." But he did not come down to join the crowd. Off we go to another meeting of the Concerned Citizens of Alaskan Mothers Against Cannikin, and another round of speeches, Bohlen getting to his feet patiently and starting at A for Arms Race, B for Bombs in General, C for Cannikin, the whole scene all over again.

TUESDAY, OCTOBER 26, 1971

From Juneau we travel down the Inside Passage, through mazes of the channels and narrows and straits of the Alaska panhandle to the city of Ketchikan. Another anti-Amchitka demonstration, another town meeting, more speeches – "Man," says Keziere, "this political campaign scene can get awfully goddamn tiring" – and down to Prince Rupert, touching at last on Canadian soil. Yet another wild round of meetings, speeches, hitting the bars, being taken off to interviews with newspapers and television and radio, phoning in columns and stories. Everybody is completely punchy and exhausted by this time, but at each port, a new wave of people comes surging aboard, their energy crashing around us like new storms with wild vibrations of bracing energy.

Slowly it dawns on us that the battle of Amchitka may have only begun. The newspapers are full of headlines about the test, environmentalists are launching fresh, stronger-than-ever legal attacks, demonstrations are mounting in intensity all across Canada. U.S. consulates are under siege from Vancouver to Fredericton, the border has been blockaded again, there are threats to bomb American-owned companies if Cannikin goes off. . . . At each stop the excitement grows, because it seems that the Megamachine is being slowed, and maybe it *will* be halted.

Still, the excitement seems somehow abstract. By now I have only one constant throbbing attitude – cynicism. So cynical I want to throw up. The question that has not yet been answered still tangles my mind in webs of glue: why did we turn around? Was it because Bohlen and Metcalfe's egos could not let go of the boat? Or was it my own ego that could not let go? The questioning is bottomless, like a searchlight going down down into a great sea canyon, everything getting murkier and murkier. Ego, ego, ego. Everything seems to come down to this – the endless clashing of egos, helpless as pendulums to stop the perpetual motion. Too long we have lived on top of one another, too stripped away are our defences, too naked we walk among each other. Now I consider all words to be bullshit, all statements to be lies, all communication to have been a blind struggling of crazed wills turned against each other. We are not so far above the crabs and the cats and the whales and the porpoises and the birds. We are nearly as powerless as they to resist the hidden engines that drive us.

But in Alert Bay the mood peaks, then breaks, and I am once again free to be stupid enough to have hope. Alert Bay – a crowd of forty people have gathered on the dock to greet us. Thurston wraps himself in the Alaskan flag the police chief gave us at Kodiak and I throw an American flag over my shoulders, and off the boat we bound, marching into town like high priests of some kinky cult, as strange among the townspeople as aliens, or sorcerers, or madmen. Wild clowns – that's

Hunter in Alert Bay, British Columbia.

what we are. Merry Pranksters of the environmental movement. "You two loonies at it again?" Cormack says. We are indeed, but only for a short while. Within an hour we have shed our flag-capes and entered a whole new place, like sideshow freaks entering a cathedral.

We are taken into the longhouse, a wooden building about the size of a barn whose entire front wall is adorned by a Kwak'waka'wakw crest, a creature within creatures within creatures. The great totem poles with their strange other-dimensional faces hold up massive wooden beams, a fire of cedar wood flares, smoke drifts everywhere, women in blood-red beaded robes dance, and old men with hands like roots beat a great wooden drum persistently, with the patience of calling birds. Here the Greenhawks stand in a silent row, tiny beneath the overhanging carved beaks of thunderbirds, whose wings are spread into fans as they prepare to leap into the sky. The mighty Greenhawks are not sure what to do. Look at them – each stands in a different way, Simmons as though waiting his turn at the fountain of youth, Bohlen with his head bowed (he finally does look like a Quaker), Hunter with his hair combed like an altar boy and his hands crossed in front of him, Marining a shaggy prophet, Moore a little kid standing awestruck before a towering grandfather, Cummings an oddly innocent 1950s greaser with slicked-back hair, Metcalfe with his feet planted apart and arms across his chest, Thurston a wise old mandarin who has finally reached the doorway to the last truth, Darnell almost a Boy Scout standing at attention, Birmingham attentive but expecting a lecture from the teacher. Even old John Cormack joins the lineup, walking forward shyly, covering his shyness with the grumpiest face imaginable. And Keziere, caught in the schizophrenic demands of his technological art, works behind his camera for long minutes, freezing the moment in time. For this may be a significant moment. This may be the taking-from of the vision of Eyes of Fire. The Warriors of the Rainbow stand in the confusion of a new experience, and it is mystical – as mystical as the

In the Kwak'wa̱ka'wakw longhouse at Alert Bay, British Columbia.

eco-cairn on Akutan Mountain, as mystical as the flung-down cathedral of the ocean, as mystical as the Greenpeace Church, as mystical as the disintegrating totem poles along the B.C. coast. Somehow everything is coming into focus.

Lying on the ground outside, ready to be lifted into position, is the largest totem pole in the world – 178 feet long. In a sacred ritual normally reserved for weddings, funerals, and the election of chiefs, each of us is made a brother of the Kwak'waka'wakw people. We are asked to remove our hats and there we stand, a bunch of bedraggled unshaven establishment hippies and space-age technicians, many of us on the verge of crying as our heads are anointed with water and white feathers from the dove, which the Kwak'waka'wakw, too, understand as the symbol of peace. It is a religious experience.

Daisy Sewid, daughter of Chief Jimmy Sewid, presides over the ceremonies, which include three dances by Kwak'waka'wakw women that hold a special meaning for the crew of the *Greenpeace*. The first is a dance that encourages people to let go of their egos, lest their egos grow so large and monstrous that they are turned into cannibals. The second dance symbolizes a journey at sea. And the third dance, which we are invited to join after being wrapped in Kwak'waka'wakw robes, is simply a dance of peace, in which the dove feathers on our headdresses are allowed to drift through the air, touching everyone present.

WEDNESDAY, OCTOBER 27, 1971

And then we are moving down the coast, humming "We love you, Greenpeace, Oh yes we do. . . ." Forty-two days we have been on this trip. And the news comes through from Vancouver that Nixon has finally made himself perfectly clear. Cannikin will be detonated on about November 4. Today is October 27. If we had stayed in Sand

Point until the end of October, as Fineberg and Simmons and Darnell and I wanted to do, we would now be in a position to make the run to Amchitka. As it is, we are about 2,000 miles away. No words are exchanged as we press together in the radio room and the Penthouse, listening to the news, but like a crackling psychic grid, the mood in the boat flares back into the anger and outrage that burned at Sand Point. This is one more smack in the face – a new layer of numbness has been laid on top of all the other layers of numbness. We look around at one another, the thought growing in several minds at once: can we try again? No sooner has the collective notion begun to take form than the room fills with low moans. To go through all of that again? The ego, which is still monstrous, reminds us of Cummings' pointed remark back in Sand Point at the last meeting: "We'll look pretty silly sailing under the Lions Gate Bridge in Vancouver as Cannikin goes off."

And now, the final grand piano. Dorothy announces over the radio that a converted minesweeper, the *Edgewater Fortune*, is being readied by the Don't Make a Wave Committee in Vancouver, and within a day it will launch itself in a mad run up the Inside Passage and across the Gulf of Alaska in the hopes of arriving in time to be standing three miles from Amchitka when the bomb goes off. All night, she says, the phones rang as volunteers called up from all over western Canada. Some 400 people are willing to take a run. The boat will be renamed the *Greenpeace Too*.

"*What?*" screams Thurston.

Coming up on us fast in the grey dawn is the *Edgewater Fortune*. It is as though the *Confidence* has come back to haunt us, a military ship bearing down on us in the wet cold rainy gloom.

"Look at that big mother," says Keziere.

"Oh lovely, lovely," says Bohlen.

"Isn't that nice," grins Moore.

"Is that on *our* side?" asks Cummings.

The *Greenpeace* alongside the *Greenpeace Too* at Comox, British Columbia.

The crews of the *Greenpeace* and the *Greenpeace Too*. From left: Darnell, Hunter, Gerry Deiter, unknown cameraman, Chris Bergthorson, Birmingham, Captain Henry Johansen.

"This is certainly somethin', ain't it now?" says Birmingham.

We stand in the piddling rain and cold, cheering. The cheers are amazingly hoarse. The boat slides effortlessly up to us, looming larger and larger until the men on the *Edgewater Fortune* are looking down at us as from a tall building.

"Hey, man," says Marining, "I'm suffering from Future Shock. First time."

A minesweeper. It looks like Canada has finally declared war on the United States of America. But it's too choppy out here in the waters of the Strait of Georgia. The *Greenpeace Too* backs off and heads toward Comox, on Vancouver Island. Like a grubby old rubber duck, the *Greenpeace* bounces along in her wake. (Ah, but Phyllis, it was you who got that thing in motion.) At Comox we pull in beside the minesweeper, and there is a mad flurry of handshakes and hugs. This hulking giant castle of a warship seems to have a crowd aboard, including some familiar faces. They take pictures of us as Keziere goes on determinedly clicking his own little camera at them. It is like the old days, when the Hercules boomed its cinematic cannons at us. The media war goes on – the CBC has a crew of cameramen aboard, and tough old Doug Collins, a journalist who broke out of some dozen Nazi prison camps during the war, and local radio announcers, and a *Vancouver Sun* reporter, Jim McCandlish, to replace me. Climbing aboard that supercraft after six weeks on our little halibut seiner is a bit like visiting a spaceship. You could pick up the *Phyllis Cormack* and stuff her in the hold without slowing down the larger boat by a knot.

Everybody aboard moves with a sense of urgency – they have less than a week to travel 2,400 miles across that gale-haunted Gulf to Amchitka – so we rush our greetings, our interviews, our handshakes, and we rush to pull down the ragged Greenpeace flag and pass it over. They run it up their flagpole immediately, a flag representing peace and ecology being run up the mast of a minesweeper! The war movie atmosphere saturates the moment. *World War Three!* It is finally happening. Down from the galley wall comes the poster of the mushroom cloud, down comes the *Friendship Frigate* poster, and out comes the Geiger counter. We hand them over, along with all the extra boots, jackets, sweaters, and gloves we can find lying around. The new crew of twenty-eight have not had much time to pack, having been selected from the hundreds of applicants only ten hours before the ship pulled out. Simmons, Cummings, Marining, and Birmingham volunteer to transfer to the *Greenpeace Too*. Cormack wants to go too, but he can't – skippers don't share their command with other skippers, and Captain Hank Johansen of the *Edgewater Fortune* is not likely to break with tradition.

For the rest of us, this is the last torture rack to survive – deciding whether to climb on-board the second boat and keep right on going. It is a dance that encourages people to let go of their egos. The ego howls, *Goooooooo!* But the ego is isolated now and cut off from some of the controls. For a moment, Metcalfe, Bohlen, Darnell, and I stand facing each other, the old ego-conflicts exploding in a sunburst – If you go, I'll have to go – which breaks when we all grab hands and Bohlen shouts, "How far?" And we shout back, *"All the way home!"* Simmons, who has been consistent all the way, remains consistent and goes. They need an engineer, so Birmingham goes. Cummings goes. Marining climbs away, headphones slung around his neck, carrying his little white metal suitcase filled with tapes and spare batteries and games like Risk and chess. The *Greenpeace Too* sloughs away into the drizzle. And home we race.

SATURDAY, OCTOBER 30, 1971

When we arrive in Vancouver at about 7:30 p.m., we can hear car horns honking from the Lions Gate Bridge. Once again Thurston is draped in the flag of Alaska, and I wear the American flag over my shoulders like a cape. It's low tide, which means we may not be able to make it all the way into downtown Vancouver along False Creek. We all stand out on deck and strain to levitate the boat. Slowly, slowly, Cormack pushes the *Greenpeace* into the channel, eye cocked on the depth sounder, saying, "Got about one fathom clear on the bottom, nope, now she's down to nuttin', we're touching bottom. . . ." Levitate! Levitate! *Levitate!* The boat lifts herself magically over the shallows.

"First goddamn time I ever got through there when the tide's right out," says Cormack, rubbing his chin.

"Shithouse karma," says Thurston.

Then comes the wildest craziest moment of all, as we bear down on a dock jammed with a couple hundred people, all hunched up under umbrellas, looking like elves under little black mushrooms, ear-splitting squeals and cheers everywhere. My eyes rake the faces, looking for Zoe and the kids, and *there she is*, and I tear off my furry Bolshevik hat and fling it into the crowd, right at her. The boat whirls down on the dock, and for a moment everyone on the boat has a single thought: are we going to crash into the dock and kill everyone? Damn near. Snow is falling. My God, it's winter!

Moore throws out a line as the dock, with all those people on it, waving and yelling, streams by us like a subway platform at rush hour. The boat is moving awfully damn fast and Cormack is roaring at someone on the dock to get that goddamn rope around something. It dawns on us that reverse gear has failed to engage. The rope catches, whangs taut, and starts to split and splinter, but with a tortured sideways heave, the *Greenpeace* crunches heavily to a stop, half a dozen threads of string having made the difference between stopping and sailing on past the dock to crash into a concrete seawall.

Home!

SATURDAY, NOVEMBER 6, 1971

The Gulf of Alaska is still a tunnel of raving sea witches and "freak ones," moans out of the void and smoking waves, at the moment of the blast when the granite basilica is flung down like the walls of Hiroshima. Even the 154-foot *Edgewater Fortune* was forced to slow to a crawl when she hit the sleets and axe-blows of green in early November, and finally, more than half the crew laid out seasick, bodies strewn in the lounges, cabins, and passageways, Hank Johansen did what John Cormack was forced to do: "Hard around!" And they ran for it, ran in their great steel skin, ran like hell for their lives. They backed out of the Olympian ravings of the Gulf of Alaska, turned, and headed up the Inside Passage, through which the *Phyllis Cormack* had just retreated. It was a longer route, but the only opening through which the boat could pass while wind-armies held the open sea. Even moving at seventeen knots, the *Edgewater Fortune* looked to have no chance of reaching Amchitka by November 4, the scheduled date of the Cannikin blast. But the battle was still like the Great War of the Rings, and Canadians – even when they are riding winged white stallions instead of their paint-peeling old merry-go-round horsies – are still Hobbits. While the *Greenpeace Too* galloped toward the Mountains of Mordor, her crew still dreaming desperately of throwing the One Ring into the Cracks of Doom, the warriors of the Big People were locked in a Goliath's embrace back in the Field of Cormallen, Washington, D.C. No sooner did Nixon give the go-ahead on Cannikin than the legal spear-tip of the movement leapt into the courts. Meanwhile, the same storms that were preventing the *Edgewater Fortune* from charging across the Gulf in a straight line were slowing down work at the weapons shop of Amchikta. The test was delayed a day. And another day. Forward rushed the *Greenpeace Too*.

Then, on November 5, the day before Cannikin was ready to be unleashed, the Unites States Supreme Court ordered an emergency full court hearing on the test. Hundreds of thousands of clenched Canadian fists had been beating for a week against the dented battered undefended border. From the moment of the birth of *Greenpeace Too*, which rose like a phoenix from the ashes of the nest of our dreams, the only issue in Canada had been Amchitka. The largest crowds in the history of Toronto, Vancouver, Winnipeg, and Calgary turned out to stalk the streets in protest. Hardhats marched with hippies on the streets below the offices of American consulates. The bridge at Niagara Falls was plugged with thousands of fist-waving students. Down a street in Toronto marched a long phalanx of middle-aged men in stockbrokers' overcoats and black bowler hats, like a trainload of wind-up toys, bearing a sign that said STOP AMCHITKA. A group of Canadians, including Lester Pearson and Chief Dan George. took out a full-page ad in *The Washington Post*, an open letter to the American people urging that the test be cancelled. Walter Cronkite showed the Vancouver Real Estate Board anti-Amchitka commercial on national television. Thousands of pulp workers downed tools in British Columbia. Fishermen swung their boats out into the Georgia Strait, tooting their horns in protest. Carpenters and plumbers went on the march. The world's longest telegram, containing 188,000 signatures – a list half a mile long – was delivered to the White House. Members of Parliament, mayors, senators, legislators, aldermen, clergy – all stood together in the attack. The Transpolitical Environmental Alliance flickered briefly and magnificently into life. For the first time since the War of 1812, Americans were confronted with the spectre of an uprising along their naked northern flank. U.S. television coverage of the test rose abruptly from a squeak to a shrill whine, in which there was the beginning of an actual snarl.

At dawn on this day, Saturday, November 6, the *Edgewater Fortune* is approaching Sand Point, 700 miles from Ground Zero, a Canadian Air Force plane launched to the test site by Ottawa has bogged down somewhere in the Northwest Territories, the largest demonstration in Canadian history has blown through the streets of hundreds of cities, towns, and villages – and the U.S. Supreme Court has voted four to three to let the bomb go. At 9:30 a.m., the last workers hustle into their jeeps and roar away across the moonlike barrens of Amchitka and around the mountain range, and leap into their concrete bunker. Pressure has mounted so swiftly and massively that the Atomic Energy Commission has been moved to send the teenaged daughter of its chairman, James Schlesinger, up to the island with him as a publicity gimmick. "It's a nice place for a picnic for the kids," he says, giving the go to unleash a force that will flare to the temperature of the sun, triggering the largest underground blast in American history, generating a shock wave that registers 7.2 on the Richter scale, a force equal to that of the great San Francisco earthquake. The ocean around Amchitka churns like a milkshake, rocks slip down fifty-foot cliffs, whole sections of earth fall into the sea, and a crater almost a mile wide is dug into the centre of the island. The bunker containing Schlesinger, his daughter, and his technicians bucks like a cable car on its steel springs. A cavern the size of two football fields opens instantaneously in the rock. Planet Earth twitches as though stung by a mosquito.

The *Greenpeace Too* pulls in at Sand Point, her huge steel hull slamming the wharf so hard that the workers in the cannery come running out in terror, thinking the bomb has triggered an earthquake. Headlines scream, AMCHITKA N-BLAST "SAFE, SUCCESSFUL," despite the vast new socket in the wobbly bedrock of the Aleutian Islands filled with Strontium-90 and Cesium-136, a devil's brew of radioactive isotopes that will endure for thousands of years, awaiting the day when an earthquake or volcano cracks open the death chamber and spews invisible rays on our children or grandchildren or grandchildren's children.

In the instant of Cannikin's awakening, a thousand otters die in the Bering Sea, their ears split by the shock wave, and their brown wet bags of bodies wash up on the shores for weeks afterwards. Our brothers, the otters. The end.

AFTER

JUNE 2004

When I got back from the expedition to Amchitka and sat down to write a book about it, I was convinced we had lost, and I was angry. The best chance ever to actually interfere with nuclear testing, and we had blown it through sheer stupidity – and a failure of nerve, to put it kindly. *Cop-Out on the Way to Amchitka* was the title that loomed in my mind. And my personal failure of will was a big factor in that cop-out. Worse, I was afraid that I'd subconsciously thrown the fight to carry on with the voyage. I'd have to live with that until I died or the world blew up, whichever happened first.

I was also facing the most serious writing dilemma of my life. Since childhood, when I had started writing science fiction in my school scribblers, I had been looking for "experience." Like all intense young writers, I had plenty to say, but rather little context in which to present my thoughts. I'd read a bit, but there had been no plagues or crusades or recent wars on home ground. Even when the Great Red River Flood hit in 1950, my family was evacuated before the dikes broke. Real-life adventure had been hard to come by in working-class south Winnipeg after the war, a period during which Canada was at its dullest, if you can imagine. Such adventures as I'd managed to experience when I was growing up had been of the ordinary romantic or travel or childhood close-call variety. I had done some solo camping in the boreal forest and some hitchhiking in western Canada and Europe, had got married and fathered two children, had embarked on an interesting career in journalism and published three books, but until that fateful voyage in the fall of 1971, nothing had happened to me that leaped out as being absolutely essential to write about, if only for my own understanding of life. And now that it had, I was obliged *not* to write about it – for the sake of the cause.

The problem was that I'd *joined*. What exactly I'd joined was not yet clear – it was still being defined – but I had definitely stopped being on the outside looking in and was instead on the inside looking out. I'd started out as a newspaper columnist, the ultimate Ishmaelian outsider, accustomed to being responsible for nothing except the authenticity of my insights and words. "Tell it like it is" was the creed of the counterculture scribe, and my personal mantra. Suddenly I found myself in the inner circle of a nascent political organization, with a bit of potential power in my hand, which at the time seemed like the power to change the course of history. All that had to happen was for the MV *Phyllis Cormack,* AKA *Greenpeace,* to make it to Amchitka Island and park there under the nose of a nuclear test bomb code-named Cannikin. How much simpler could it be?

Yet everything got fucked up. We never quite managed to go in the direction we wanted to go, or be in the place we wanted to be. And we fought bitterly among ourselves about it. Everything we did or said got sucked into an overwhelming power struggle. Here we were, supposedly saving the world through our moral example, emulating the Quakers, no less, when in reality we spent most of our time at each other's throats, egos clashing, the group fatally divided from start to finish. As every writer since Homer could tell you, this was the story: the conflict within. But having agreed, early in the game, to the Unity Rule – something like: I Pledge to Stay On-Side With the Group No Matter What, which had seemed like a bold leap into solidarity with The Movement at the time – I had effectively gagged myself as a reporter and historian. It was a trade-off, but I had bought into it, so I couldn't complain. I'd get to be part of the consensus – my own skinny hand on the wheel of decision-making over the course of the *Greenpeace*, and therefore destiny – but like any other politician, I'd have to agree not to disagree in public. I disagreed, as it turned out, with just about everything that was done, but had to keep my mouth shut. How, therefore, to write a book? An *authorized* book, which followed the party line yet still told the awful truth – that we had screwed up.

Three decades later, his grey beard turned white, Jim Bohlen confided to me over a drink that he had been giving the sailing orders to our captain in secret throughout the voyage. As the guy signing the cheques and as the chairman of the Don't Make a Wave Committee, which had chartered the boat, Bohlen had the legal authority to do that, but rather than say that he was the boss, and that the *Greenpeace* and the protest action were therefore being run as an old-fashioned hierarchical power structure, he played games to keep us radical young crewmen under control. One of them was the promise that the ship would be run by consensus – each of us would have the power of veto. This was considered the ultimate hip form of sharing power at the time, and I, for one, respected it.

But it was all a sham. Decisions were indeed made – Bohlen made them. And he made them after the rest of us had gone back to our bunks. At the time I wrote my manuscript, immediately after the voyage, I had no idea what Bohlen had been up to behind the scenes. On any given day the actual movements of the boat, as opposed to the direction we'd agreed to at our meeting the night before, remained a mystery to me. Bohlen had us completely flummoxed. I salute him now for his cunning and maturity and prudence. We probably would have died if he hadn't assumed control. But back then, I plotted and connived to overthrow him as leader because he was "chickening out." Ben Metcalfe, Bohlen's co-conspirator in the plot to bring us home alive, the other mature war veteran on board, and the mastermind of the media campaign, saw no reason to put us at risk of committing mass suicide, and I sneered at him for having "lost it." But this guy had fought in the Desert War against Rommel, had resisted RAF orders to bomb Gandhi's followers, and was so far ahead of me in terms of that elusive stuff called experience that there was never any doubt that in matters of life or death he would outmanoeuvre the mutinous but naïve youth faction. He was an old rogue survivor. A genius, I now realize. In the end, I studied at his feet.

The man who ultimately determined the fate of that first Greenpeace trip was John C. Cormack, the captain and owner, who had accepted the job of sailing his fishing boat into a nuclear test zone only out of economic desperation, a fact that never got talked about much. In hindsight it is interesting to remember what Cormack did and did not do at the critical moment. He saved his boat and us along with it. And we all saved face, at least enough to go home.

The key moment of the trip came a day before we limped back into Vancouver. As we all sat slumped in the galley, burned out, Bohlen announced that he was going to shut down the Don't Make a Wave Committee as soon as he got the chance. It was an *ad hoc* group and it had done its thing. Don't do that, I told him. Why waste all this hard-earned media capital? Fold the committee, sure, but reconstitute it as the Greenpeace Foundation. That was my main contribution, yet the moment did not find its way into my manuscript. It was an element of hope for a future revolution, and I was not hopeful as I bobbed in the harbour at Steveston, heartsick and overmedicated, writing the story of our failure. In the end I told the truth as I saw it, supposedly as it was, never mind loyalty to the cause.

As it turned out, all my angst was unnecessary. Time has proven my post-trip despair to be utterly mistaken. The trip was a success beyond anybody's wildest dreams. That bomb went off, but the bombs planned for after that did not. The nuclear test program at Amchitka was cancelled five months after our mission, and some scholars argue that this was the beginning of the end of the Cold War. Whatever history decides about the big picture, the legacy of the voyage itself is not just a bunch of guys in a fishing boat, but the Greenpeace the entire world has come to love and hate.

Acknowledgments

Thanks to Karen Love for salvaging the copy of a forgotten manuscript, Emily Hunter for typing it into electronic form, and Mary Schendlinger for editing it into shape.

Robert Hunter, cofounder and first president of Greenpeace, was named one of the ten eco-heroes of the twentieth century by *Time* magazine. He is a veteran writer, broadcaster, and speaker on issues of the environment and climate change. He won a Governor General's Award for his 1991 book *Occupied Canada* and in 1994 was awarded the Canadian Environmental Award. He lives in Toronto.

Robert Keziere was the chief photographer at the Vancouver Art Gallery and for the past twenty years has run a freelance business specializing in the photography of art. He lives in Vancouver.

photo: Bill Darnell

Join Greenpeace

Greenpeace continues to campaign to protect our beautiful planet. Today's Greenpeace carries on the tradition of dedication and conviction that drove its founders, and continues to use non-violent creative confrontation to expose global environmental problems and to force the solutions that are essential to a green and peaceful future.

In order to maintain its independence, Greenpeace does not solicit funds from corporations or the government but relies on donations from committed individuals around the world. Join them on the frontline for the earth – become a Greenpeace supporter.

Canada	*greenpeace.ca*	800-320-7183
United States	*greenpeaceusa.org*	800-326-0959
United Kingdom	*greenpeace.org.uk*	44 207-865-8100
Germany	*greenpeace.da*	49 40-306-180
Australia	*greenpeace.org.au*	800-815-151
New Zealand	*greenpeace.net.nz*	0-800-22-33-44
Greenpeace International (Netherlands)	*greenpeace.org*	31 20-514-8150